Praise for Debrah Constance . . .

"Debrah's journey should be an inspiration and give hope to those who feel they've been dealt an unfair hand in life. A remarkable story of determination and faith."

Johnny Carson

"The remarkable Debrah Constance has been one of my great inspirations—a successful businesswoman who decided that she wanted her life to be about something larger than herself and created A Place Called Home, a haven of safety and creativity for children and teens. Her life story is heartbreaking and inspiring, filled with passion and hope. Read it and weep . . . and cheer. And be prepared to rethink your life."

Arianna Huffington
syndicated columnist and author of *Fanatics and Fools:*
The Game Plan for Winning Back America

"Debrah Constance is a hero to me. She has not only turned around the lives of thousands of children at A Place Called Home, but she's also turned around my life because she's taught me to do, not just talk. I love her very much, and I feel her story is important for America to hear."

Jasmine Guy
actress and author of
Afeni Shakur: Evolution of a Revolutionary

FAT STUPID UGLY

One Woman's Courage to Survive

Debrah Constance
founder, A Place Called Home
as told to J.I. Kleinberg

Foreword by Penny Marshall

Health Communications, Inc.
Deerfield Beach, Florida

www.hcibooks.com

Library of Congress Cataloging-in-Publication Data

Constance, Debrah, 1947–
    Fat, stupid, ugly : one woman's courage to survive / Debrah Constance; as told
to J.I. Kleinberg ; foreword by Penny Marshall.
    p. cm.
    ISBN-13: 978-0-7573-0225-1
    ISBN-10: 0-7573-0225-4
    1. Constance, Debrah, 1947–   2. Incest victims—United States—Biography.
3. Women—United States—Biography. I. Title.

HV6570.7.C66 2004
362.76'4'092—dc22
[B]

2004052281

Publisher: Health Communications, Inc.
            3201 S.W. 15th Street
            Deerfield Beach, FL 33442-8190

R-01-07

Cover photo: Debrah Constance, age eight
Cover design by Larissa Hise Henoch
Inside book design by Dawn Von Strolley Grove

For Gideon

and for the children of A Place Called Home,

who can't change the past

but can work and dream to create a better future.

And for Grandma Frances and Grandma May,

who would be so proud.

CONTENTS

ACKNOWLEDGMENTS

My life, my work and this book would not have been possible without the gracious support and guiding wisdom of a great many people.

From before the first word was written, Gary Seidler's belief in this project launched a lifetime of memories. Thyonne Gordon's untiring spirit cheered me along from beginning to end. At Health Communications, Inc., Allison Janse and Elisabeth Rinaldi patiently guided us through the editorial maze.

A Place Called Home has been a collaboration of children, staff, community and donors in numbers too great to mention here. Those whose vision made it possible to tell the stories in this book include, in particular, David L. Crippens, for asking the right question; Jon Douglas, for giving me the freedom to try something untested; Reverend Arthur Jupiter and Bishop Matthew Richardson, for believing in something unknown and taking a risk that helped thousands of children; the members of the current APCH Board, Peter M. Gilhuly, Esq., Arianna Huffington, Terrence Duckette, Jasmine Guy, Robert Davidow, Bruce Newberg, Sister Patricia Connor, RSHM, Colin Horowitz, Robert Israel, Kenneth Karmin, Peter Neuwirth, the Honorable Jan Perry, Gary Seidler, Bob Thompson and Stephen R. Winston, as well as our past board members, advisory board and gracious donors over the last eleven years, whose vision and enthusiasm keep us going; the Religious of the Sacred Heart of Mary, for their spirited support, generosity and the Gailhac Learning Program; Rabbi Jan Goldstein, for helping us to recognize and heal our sacred wounds; Thyonne Gordon, Christopher Smart, Chico Brown, Juliana Wells, Gwynne Walker (my assistant at Jon Douglas Company as well as at APCH, always at my side) and the entire APCH staff, who carry the ball; Penny Marshall, Arianna Huffington and Jasmine Guy, for unrestrained enthusiasm and kind words; and, most especially, Johnny Carson, without whom the triumphant chapters of this story might never have happened.

Among the many precious spirits in my life who have held me in the darkness and celebrated with me in the light are Charlotte and Clancy, for believing in me when I didn't believe in myself; Monique and Lawrence, for accepting and returning unconditional love; Gail Gurland, always ready with an inspired idea; my yoga mentors and healers, Ana Forrest, Forrest Yoga Circle; Bryan Kest, the king of Power Yoga; and Max Strom, owner of Sacred Movement in Venice, California; as well as Matthew Cohen, Saul David Raye, Micheline Berry, Sherry Brourman, Gianna and Venetia Carotenuto, and Jill Miller, all of whom have helped me recover and thrive; my insightful and generous nutritionist, Sabrina Balter; my doctors who wouldn't give up, who saved my life and whom I acknowledge specially here: Dr. Jim Nishimine; Dr. Soram Khalsa, the tenacious medical detective who sent me to the best people for help; Dr. Debra Judelson, heart specialist, and her assistant, Charlie, who always fit me in, no matter what; Dr. Russell Shimizu, neurologist extraordinaire; and Dr. Sibel Kar, who took care of my heart and found a place for APCH in his. Thanks also to Bunny Chamberlin for her loving heart and special skill as my respiratory therapist.

My world would be a drab, gray place without Sister Patricia Connor, RSHM, my anchor in a storm, always listening, always trusting, always understanding; Sharon Gedan, whose wisdom has shined a great light into my life; my dear, precious, beautiful, brilliant sisters, Wendy and Victoria, whose stories are different from mine, and whose support, friendship and love are as important as breath itself; and my son, my angel, Gideon, who has lived half of this story at my side and whose capacity for love and forgiveness surpasses even a proud mother's fondest hopes.

To J.I., whose voice is my voice and whose friendship is everlasting, I am immeasurably grateful.

The shape of my life and this book have been inspired, illuminated and blessed in more ways than I can possibly express by my Diana. Her attention, grace and humor have helped me fill the lapses in my memory, animate my stories and polish my words. Without her, these stories, this book and my life would be meaningless.

FOREWORD

Even from the outside, A Place Called Home is something different. In a neighborhood scarred with graffiti, APCH is big, bright, white and unmarked. But it's not until you turn off South Central Avenue and drive through the entrance gate that you begin to feel the true energy of the place. First you notice a group of youngsters intently putting the final touches on a vibrant mural. Then you hear the sounds of kids playing a fast game of basketball. There's a buzz of children's voices in the patio, and once you walk through the door, the buzz turns into a happy uproar. Beneath high ceilings, the huge, colorful recreation area reverberates with the clamor of movie soundtracks, video games, clattering pool balls and laughter.

Walk into one room and you find children working on art projects; in another you discover dancers perfecting new moves, intently focused on the directions of their instructor. In the music studio, you might get to hear young rap artists rehearsing their latest number or a teenager practicing classical guitar.

But APCH is not all about noise. There are quiet places where children study, work with tutors, and get counseling. In a community where gang membership is almost assumed, APCH offers an intensive and supportive program to help the children find better ways to live. Every child is treated with dignity and respect, every dream is taken seriously and every success is applauded.

A Place Called Home sprang from the imagination of Debrah Constance, who tells her colorful and unconventional story in these pages. The need for such a place— and dozens like it—is indisputable. But to assemble a devoted paid and volunteer staff, to build and maintain unique programs, to continually attract new donors and to keep the whole operation going, through good times and bad, for nearly eleven years, is a tribute to Debrah's passion and a gift to the community.

It is an honor to be a part of A Place Called Home.

—*Penny Marshall, Director*

AUTHOR'S NOTE

I began life, it would seem, as some kind of Grimm's fairy tale creature, large and oafish, undesirable, grossly imperfect. Neatly penned in my baby book were the words, "Debbie was a fat, unattractive baby."

Fat and ugly aside, my life was fairly normal for the first couple of years. During that uncomplicated time, I could have set out on any of a dozen different paths toward an orderly life. Found my way to happiness without significant chaos or pain. But it was not to be.

Before I could talk, the abuse began, followed by a haunting succession of smoking and pills, rage and rebellion, alcoholism, cancer and broken marriages. The path I took was rutted and slippery, dark and twisted, looping back on itself in unmarked detours.

But this is not a story of defeat. This is a book about surviving. It's about hope. It's about the amazing resilience of the human spirit. It's about how each of us—ordinary, imperfect, damaged—can dream and empower and heal.

The stories in this book are true. They have many characters—a few recognizable, many disguised. If some of these people injured me along the way, I have little doubt that I caused them pain as well. I have made every attempt to write with honesty and without blame, to cast aside self-pity, and to discover and share the lessons—and the humor—that have helped me survive.

And make no mistake: surviving is full-time work. The path still twists and plunges off in uncharted directions. But I'm better at watching where I put my feet, and I know that if I get in trouble, there's always someone who will reach out a hand and help me through the next patch of swamp or over the next impassable wall.

—Debrah Constance, May 2004

INTRODUCTION:
COMING OUT OF THE CLOSET

My closet isn't a figure of speech. It's a real place. Many real places.

The closet was the place where I hid from my father. Hid from his loud, accusing voice. Hid my body from his hands. The closet was my safety zone, my real home, a tiny haven where I could be invisible.

It was the most important room in the house.

Through my early and difficult years, Grandma Frances was my favorite person in the world. She was loving and kind to me. Her closet was full of silky things that smelled wonderful. She hanged herself there.

On the escape route from my first husband, I crossed the country and changed my name. But that wasn't enough. In my apartment, I lived in the closet. Into the womb-room safety of its red walls and black carpeting, I retreated after work to eat and sleep.

During my detox in 1985, I tried to hide from my demons in the tiny, cramped closet in my hospital room. Other patients would come into my room and knock on the closet door to urge me to come out. Terrified, I refused; I preferred the dark.

Even after years of therapy and a year of sobriety, I found myself crouched in the closet after my sponsor informed me that it was my turn to lead an A.A. meeting. She thought she was offering me a big prize for my milestone celebration; I only felt a terror that kept me huddled in the dark for a whole day.

By that time, I had seen a lot of closets, both personally and professionally. I had been working in real estate for a number of years and had toured some of the grandest estates in Beverly Hills. But as far as I was concerned, they could keep their views and swimming pools, their country kitchens and palatial bathrooms. I only coveted their closets.

One day about eight years ago, I was sitting in a coffee shop with a friend. I told her that I had decided to go to my first Overeaters Anonymous (O.A.) meeting. Then I went on to tell her about my life in closets and how closets had always been my safest place. A woman at the next table leaned over and said, "I couldn't help overhearing you mention closets. I'm redesigning the closets in my house. I wonder if you know a good closet person." Now this was in Los Angeles, where a lot of people "know a good closet person," but I didn't. Thinking, *Who is this person who would interrupt a private conversation,* I turned back to my friend.

But as we were leaving the coffee shop, out on the street, I found myself walking right behind the eavesdropper as I made my way toward the nearby O.A. meeting. I asked whether she was also going to the meeting, and she said yes, in fact she was leading the meeting, and if I'd like to, I could sit with her. She asked about the tattoo on my wrist—a bracelet of dancing children from the logo of A Place Called Home, the youth center I founded and operated in South Central Los Angeles. So I pulled out my business card, and when she looked at it she was incredulous. She said, "I have a T-shirt with that logo sitting in my closet; I wear it all the time!" Now it was my turn for incredulity. We introduced ourselves. Her name was Diana, and although I had never met her, I immediately recognized her name. "You're one of our donors. I sent you that T-shirt myself!" Now she's my partner in life and my best friend. But that's another story.

For me, coming out of the closet was not solely a matter of sexual identity. It has been a process of finding ways to comfort myself without hiding. It has been a matter of facing my fears and learning to transform them into tools for growth. I know the closet is there and that it will always welcome me. But there's so much to do: so many children to help, not least the damaged child within myself. The closet is about *not* doing, about *not* being seen, about being safe. To help the children, to heal myself and to learn to trust, I have to be visible, to tell my story, to take risks. I have to be out of the closet.

BEGINNING

Mother labored for twelve hours, the doctor gave a yank with the forceps and I came squalling into the world on January 18, 1947. Cleaned up and ready for a little maternal affection, I was given the cold shoulder. "Take that baby away!" Mother insisted, much to the alarm and disapproval of the hospital attendants. Whether exhausted, afraid or just dismayed by my appearance, she wasn't ready to hold me.

A baby nurse was waiting for us at home in Manhattan, so if Mother didn't want to touch me for a while, at least I wouldn't suffer from lack of attention. Eventually Nan accommodated herself to motherhood, taking copious notes of my visitors, gifts and modest accomplishments. "At 15 months Deb is such a happy and outgoing baby that everyone comments on it. She loves people & gives her toys to everyone. She doesn't have any temper at all with her playmates—just loves them and laughs at everything they do." "Deb is very lovable—kisses on the least provocation—hugs her mommy all day—laughs over nothing at all. Is altogether the most wonderful baby in the world, & I was never so contented & happy."

In spite of the label—"fat, unattractive"—that I seemed to be born with and that Mother had inscribed in my baby book, things were good for a while. My parents, Nan and Arnold, took me for walks in Central Park, tended to my needs and shuffled me from place to place as they changed addresses. Nan was petite and beautiful, a Broadway actress until she became pregnant with me. Arnold was handsome and intense, an artist and an advertising executive on Madison Avenue. A stunning couple.

If their first effort at making a picture-perfect baby had yielded disappointing results, they had much better luck the second time. Wendy, born when I was two and a half, was beautiful, a cherub, perfect in every way. Within months, her ideal beauty was confirmed: Wendy was chosen and photographed as a Gerber baby.

Now the toddler and big sister, I lost my position as baby. But more than that, my parents, and especially my father, had a basis for comparison. From birth, it seemed, my tiny precocious sister excelled at everything. She had beauty, talent and brains. What I did, she did better, sooner and more gracefully; what I couldn't do, she mastered without effort. All of my parents' pride and attention swirled around her as Wendy became their "real" daughter, and I became the "other," swept along in the wake of her accomplishments. This was a game that I could never win. I had been born Fat and Ugly and no quantity of kisses or laughter could erase that unfortunate, and lingering, fate.

Once, when I was around seven, Wendy and I went into the city with our father to spend the day. We got to Arnold's office, and he left me sitting in a large coat closet, directing me to stay there, while he took Wendy around to meet his colleagues. Little Wendy, five years old, stood on a desk and recited the entire Gettysburg Address. He was so proud of her and so embarrassed by me, an attitude that I believed was fully justified because I was Fat, Ugly and, now by comparison with my brilliant baby sister, Stupid.

Like everyone else, I adored Wendy, doted on her and blamed myself for my own shortcomings. Our young lives were filled with music and dancing lessons, visits with loving grandparents and a continual parade of pets. Wendy was a cello prodigy, playing a miniature instrument that had belonged to a prince, but even private lessons with esteemed tutors couldn't turn me into a violin player. I was terrible and retreated to the attic for my hours of practice. Eventually I switched to the piano and was able to play decently.

We led a normal, even a privileged, life.

Except for the things that my father was doing to me.

ARNOLD

My father was a wild man—dramatic, obsessive and passionate. He made no small gestures. He had the swagger of a handsome man and a favorite son.

Growing up in the Williamsburg section of Brooklyn in an observant Jewish family, Arnold graduated early from high school and went off to study art in New York City. He served as a first lieutenant in the Air Force in World War II, and when he returned to New York at age twenty-two, he met Nan and captured her heart. Arnold in uniform, Nan a Broadway beauty—the pictures of them are dazzling.

Arnold went to work in advertising, harnessing his creativity to the cause of cigarette sales. And he continued to paint. He was enormously productive, painting through the night, lining the living room walls with artwork. His paintings were skillful, expressive and very popular. He would sell them while they were still wet.

He had a great sense of humor and loved to be the center of attention, regaling his friends with tales of wartime heroics and his imagined travels in Africa. If a story could be embellished—or an audience captured—with exaggeration and bravado, the truth be damned. He drank, smoked, shopped and lived with a passion.

Arnold owned fast cars, motorcycles and a boat. One day, Mother and I walked into the bank and caught him with wads of cash in his hands. He had just cashed his bonus check so that he could buy a second boat. Astonished, knowing nothing of his plans, Nan confronted him. Laughing with abandon, Arnold threw the fistfuls of money up in the air. He was larger than life.

Another time, we all drove into the city to a magnificent Manhattan high-rise to visit Mother's Aunt Fay. She was very dramatic, very rich, wore beautiful clothes and had a mesmerizing collection of dolls, which, I was dismayed to discover, were just for looking, not for touching. Arnold was doing his best to ingratiate her in the hope that he might inherit some of her money. But when she died, in spite of her Jewish heritage, she left all of her money to the Catholic church and was buried with her dolls. She left my father a little trinket made of elephant ivory.

When my father went shopping, anything could come home with him. One time he brought home an ocelot, but it was too wild even for Arnold. I remember him going out onto the screened porch with a stick and a chair, like a lion tamer, trying to get the big cat into a cage. (He replaced it with a more mild-mannered ocelot, Iago, who lived with us for years.) Another time, Mother told Arnold that she wanted a little bird for the gorgeous gilded birdcage that was built into the kitchen, so he went out shopping and came home with a couple of birds. Then he went out and got a few more, and a few more, until there were *dozens* of them: parrots, cockatiels, parakeets, finches, canaries and who knows what else. They'd get out of their cages and fly all over the house and into his studio, where they'd get mired in the wet oils of his latest painting.

But long before the ocelots and the birds, Arnold had introduced a monster into our household that he would show only to me: sexual abuse. Cajoling me with professions of love and promises of secrecy, he touched me in ways that nobody should touch a child. I remember being in the car with my father, sitting alongside him on the front seat. I'm small enough that my little legs stick out straight in front of me, perhaps three years old, and I am very uncomfortable. I don't understand what Arnold's hands are doing to me, only that it's something bad, and I don't like it. But he calls me his special girl, and I just keep staring at the rounded toes of my shiny black shoes.

From my earliest memories, my childhood is haunted by recurring episodes of pain and confusion at Arnold's hands. Alone with him in the den or the car, I learned my most damaging lessons about love—that it was a sinister union of affection and pain, secrecy and lies, hate and anger, powerlessness and something that I could never talk about with anyone. Ever.

There were two sides to Arnold's behavior toward me: private and public. Reserving every trace of his twisted affection for the times that we were alone, when he would tell me that he loved me as he abused me, he also made me the public target of his physical, verbal and psychological abuse.

If Mother served lovely meals and fed us plenty of vitamins, she seldom did anything to protect me from my father. She acted like she was one of the children, steering clear of Arnold's fury, noticing only the actions and words that were directed at her. When Arnold phoned home from the office, Mother would eagerly recount Wendy's achievements and my defeats—dropping a cup, not cleaning up my room, doing badly on a test, missing a dental appointment. Thus provoked, Arnold would have a few cocktails after work, ride the train home from the city, storm into the house, kick the dog, then kick me. Raving, he would yell at me, slapping me with his hand or lashing me with a towel repeatedly. He called me names, constantly reminding me that I was "Fat, Stupid, Ugly," and continued to mete out the punishment for my innate failures as well as my daily transgressions.

I tried *very* hard to be good. I'd help with the housework and try to follow the rules. But my labels—Fat, Stupid, Ugly—had already taken over, and everything I did fulfilled the prophecy of those words. I failed, Mother hid and Arnold raged. Even Wendy was more protective, throwing her small body over mine, telling Arnold to hit her, not me.

If Arnold didn't yell at me before dinner, he tormented me at the table. Mother would say, "Dinnertime," and we would all sit down at her lovely table for a moment or two of peace before Arnold continued his assault. Countless family meals were fraught with hysterics, both at home and in restaurants. I escaped from the table as soon as I could, taking my food to bed with me and eating it under the covers.

I remember one time the family was visiting my grandparents. Arnold was napping on the couch. I was sitting at the opposite end of the couch, daydreaming, thinking how much Arnold loved me, how happy I was and what a wonderful daddy he was. When Arnold woke up and saw me sitting there, he kicked me, hard, clear off the couch and said, "What are you doing here, you fat, ugly thing!" Somebody yelled at him that time, maybe my mother or my grandmother. "Don't talk to Debbie that way!" "Shut up!" he responded. This was the public side of his "affection."

The message was clear: I was Fat, Stupid and Ugly, and deserved the treatment I got, in public and in private. I was no better than a dog. I remember Arnold leaving the house with the dogs and coming back without them. Tired of their company, he had driven them out to the country and set them loose. The dogs were luckier than I was. *My* only escape was the closet—or the closet-like shelter of my blankets.

Deeply hungry for Arnold's approval, I found it only in our nightly encounters, which became a long-standing ritual. I would wake up in the middle of the night and go downstairs to sit with Arnold. He watched TV, smoked, molested me and told me that I was his friend; I was his special girl. We shared a secret that no one else could ever know: he *loved* me. It was a love constructed of anger, violence and perverse affection—a bitter legacy for his first-born daughter.

HAPPY AS A FIDDLE

In my baby book, in her neat script, Mother noted a report from my first-grade teacher: "Deb very maternal toward smaller children & new children."

From earliest memory, there was no limit to the love I felt for something small, young and helpless, whether it was my baby sisters, house pets, schoolmates or dolls. My first "baby" was Tiny Tears, a doll without a name that I could hold in my arms for hours and hours. I rocked her the way I wanted to be rocked, fed her lovingly and treated her just the way I wanted to be treated. I never hit her, called her names or hurt her body. I loved her and knew she loved me in return.

After that, there was a series of Ginny dolls—little pre-Barbie, round-faced, eight-inch beauties with eyes that opened and closed. I acted out elaborate dramas of loving motherhood, dressing them from a wardrobe of tiny out-fits sewn by my mother. (Appearances were important;

11

though Mother seemed unable to defend me against my father's assaults, she took pains to assure that everyone was nicely dressed, including the dolls.) These dolls were my friends and my perfect family.

In my imagination, in my room, in the comforting tent beneath my blankets, I tried to console myself, picture an ideal family and reconcile my father's confounding behavior. After Wendy was born, Mother cared for me, but offered me no affection or encouragement, reserving her extravagant praise and love for Wendy. For parental love, I had Arnold's secret declarations. If I found anything uplifting in his words, I was frightened and humiliated by both his public and private abuses. I hated him. But he said he loved me, and I needed his love. Time away from him was a relief. Camp and visits to grandparents offered me the only respite from his daily—and nightly—assaults and probably saved me from total emotional breakdown.

If my father's menacing presence continually pulled me toward destruction, the unquestioning love of my grandparents tugged me back to some measure of normalcy. Arnold's mother, Grandma May, and her second husband, Grandpa Louie, lived in Brooklyn, and I loved them very much. Grandpa Louie manufactured cashmere coats and gave us beautiful ones that shielded us with warmth and softness against the east coast winters.

Grandma May took me to visit her sisters, where we ate, ate, ate. We'd ride the subway and buses to downtown Manhattan to see a movie or to watch the skaters at Rockefeller Center. She would sometimes take me to temple. I don't know if they were Orthodox Jews, but they did keep kosher, with separate dishes for meat and milk foods. Now and then I'd put something on the wrong plate, and Grandma May would grab the dish, run down the stairs and bury it in the yard.

According to Mother's notes, I walked on my toes and danced as soon as I could stand, so lots of dancing lessons followed. Mother took us into the city to see the ballet, and I would come home imitating the ballerina, Maria Tallchief. When I was seven, the family moved to Great Neck, Long Island, and my sister Victoria was born. Already a practiced older sister and an abused daughter, I wanted to take care of that precious little baby and give her the affection I never got. I watched over her like a mother bear. I adored her.

More than anything, I wanted to protect her from Arnold. Fortunately, she didn't need my protection. Like Wendy and Mother, she was small and beautiful, bright and talented, and never touched by Arnold's fury—or his dangerous affection. I learned that I could leave the house knowing that she was safe.

Around the time Victoria was born, I started ice-skating. From dance, and my early acquaintance with roller-skating, it was an easy transition to ice-skating, and I loved it immediately. I loved the music, the speed and the heady feeling of freedom. I loved being alone on the ice, where, for hours at a time, I could forget that I was fat and ugly and even experience moments of beauty and grace. Skating had no connection with my father at all.

From age two onward, for a couple of months every summer, I went off to Milwaukee to stay with Mother's parents, Frances and Irving. Once I had started skating, Grandma Frances would drop me off at the rink with my lunch, and I would spend the entire day taking private and group lessons and skating, skating, skating. I had pretty little skating outfits and custom-fitted Riedell skates, and in my mind I was preparing for a professional life on the ice. I practiced my jumps and my edges and competed before the judges, but there was nothing I enjoyed more than showing off for Grandma Frances. She was always so proud of me.

I had one bad accident. Doing a huge jump, I landed with my knee on the rail and the skate blade in my butt. But nothing could keep me off the ice for long.

Grandma Frances had been a party girl. She drank and sang and smoked and throughout her life had struggled with mental illness—a struggle she eventually lost. But when I visited her, she was consistently loving, generous and kind. Wherever we went, whatever store we went into, whether it was a grocery store or Saks or Marshalls in Milwaukee, everybody knew and loved Frances.

It was during those long and healing summers that I came under the spell of Minnie, Grandma Frances' maid. When I wasn't skating or out somewhere with Grandma, I was trailing after Minnie. With her smooth, brown skin and her soft bosom, she was the very essence of safety and love. I would follow her into the basement and cuddle up to her while she ironed. She smelled like clean, warm clothes. Minnie would take me into Grandma's closet and let me try on the high heels and feel the soft fabrics. We would hang laundry or rake leaves together in the backyard and sit together on the front step. Her great warm hugs always said that life would be okay. From the time I was two until I was fourteen, Grandma and Minnie were my best friends.

When I was nine years old, my parents sent me off to a Jewish camp in Connecticut. I don't remember much about it, except saying prayers before breakfast and having bagels, lox and cream cheese in our bunkrooms on Sunday morning. Mainly I was happy to be away from home.

The next few summers, there was Camp Red Wing, which I loved. I sent a letter home describing my many activities—swimming, tennis, dramatics, woodcraft, archery, golf, sailing and horseback riding. To help me catch up where I lagged in my schoolwork, there was a tutor for me during one rest period and homework during the other.

I competed ferociously and won awards and trophies, and every summer I would excel in something that I thought would make my father love me. I needed to be the best. I would be the best tennis player, the best swimmer. One summer I labored for hours every day to learn how to fold sails and tie dozens of knots, earning a license to solo in a small sailboat. My father's daughter: he had a boat; I would be a fine sailor. I was so excited to show off my new, hard-won skills. When my parents visited, I took them out on the lake. There was no wind. All that studying, all that hoping, and no wind. The little boat just sat there. Arnold swore at me, telling me how stupid I was, that I didn't know anything. He grabbed on to the rudder and left me clutching my familiar shame. The approval I had longed for never came.

Each summer, for a little while, whether I was at camp or with my grandparents, I was able to distance myself from the ugly realities of life at home. I made a few friends and discovered that, in spite of my stupidity, I could be good at some things. I would return home ready for the rigors of another school year and toughened against Arnold's abuse.

WHERE THERE'S SMOKE . . .

Whether my father's assaults on my childhood weighed on his conscience in any way, I'll never know. As hard as I tried, I continually failed to turn myself into someone he could love. But in one subject I excelled, the perfect student: Arnold's nightly lessons in cigarette smoking.

Already committed to making cigarettes seductive to the public, Arnold brought the campaign home. He was a fiendish smoker himself, never without a cigarette, and our nightly encounters were always veiled in smoke.

Not surprisingly, my first experimental backyard smoke, when I was about ten, made me dizzy. But then, everything associated with Arnold was dizzying, and if emulating him would make me more lovable, it was a small price to pay.

By the time I was eleven, I was smoking regularly. In the middle of the night, Arnold and I smoked together in the den. He schooled me in the proper ways to hold a cigarette and how to blow smoke rings. He talked to me and was nice to me and smoked with me and did unspeakable things to me. Wasn't this proof that he loved me? The smoking, which was a clear demonstration of our twisted affection, simply became one more element in the secret that we shared.

During the day, I practiced piano in the already smoky den. I'd sit at the upright with an ashtray nearby and a cigarette dangling from my lips. But once I had stubbed out the cigarette, I couldn't leave the butt in the ashtray as evidence, so I'd quickly shove it behind the music holder. Mother caught me smoking at the piano many times, but it wasn't until Tchaikovsky developed a smoker's cough that the piano tuner, and Mother, discovered the extent of my subterfuge: *hundreds* of cigarette butts had fallen inside the piano, packed themselves beneath the keys, and dropping down further, piled up beneath the pedals until the pedals jammed, useless.

If I had to conceal the source of my cigarettes and my smoking expertise, smoking now became a badge of defiance. I sneaked smokes at camp and in school and even at Grandma Frances' house, where my smoke blended with hers and often went unnoticed. One summer, when I was eleven, Arnold packed me off to camp with cartons of Benson & Hedges in my trunk. I savored every clandestine inhale and exhale for several weeks until I was caught and my cigarettes confiscated. I was suspended from school for smoking in the bathroom.

But none of it mattered because I knew: smoking equaled love.

∞

SCHOOL DAZE

Although it got me out of the house, school was a nightmare. Every day brought further confirmation of what we already knew: Debbie is stupid.

It was hard for me to concentrate, and reading seemed too difficult. On top of the nightly disruption of my sleep for secret visits with Arnold, I was probably dyslexic. But that was before such things were diagnosed, so I muddled along from grade to grade.

Feeling self-confident after camp or a summer with Grandma, I started each fall semester with A's and B's. Once, at the beginning of the new year, I even won a spelling bee in my French class. But by the end of the term I'd be getting C's, D's and an occasional F. The moment I started to fail, I'd give up and fail completely. I sat in my chair and daydreamed, never did my homework and guessed my way through every test.

Tutors were hired in a constant but useless attempt to

keep me current, and sometimes, to my humiliation, my little sister Wendy would be engaged to coach me through painful sessions of math or English.

Compounding the other difficulties I had in school, my classmates teased me and called me "No Neck," and I began to see that my neck was an element of my ugliness that I could really focus on. Unlike other people—*everyone* else, as far as I could see—I had no clearly defined jaw line. My neck descended from my chin to my collarbone in a fleshy sort of thing that never went away.

Being aware of a clearly identifiable feature of my ugliness, I became even more self-conscious and embarrassed about it. I'd pull up my collar and, like a turtle, attempt to pull my neck and face into its concealing cover. Though, to me, my neck was awful from every direction, it seemed most awful in profile, and I often put my hand on my chin or in front of my neck in an attempt to hide it.

Because I felt so ugly, I was even too ashamed to walk up to the counter at the school library and check out books, so as an adolescent, I would simply take them home. I don't remember how long this went on, or if I ever read the books, but eventually they'd end up in the cupboard beside my bed.

One night Mother came in and discovered my huge cache of library books. She went crazy and said she was so ashamed: I would have to return all the books in the morning. I was frantic. I went into her bathroom, swallowed a bunch of sleeping pills, went to sleep and—to my great horror—woke up the next morning.

Armload by armload, I carried all the books to her car. When we got to school, Mother found a shopping cart, and we filled it to the top with books. We walked what seemed like miles from the parking lot to the library to return them. It was raining, and Mother carried an umbrella. But the very worst, most humiliating part of the experience was that Mother had made me wear my galoshes. I had to do what felt like my death march in the world's ugliest footwear.

As I entered puberty, my compliance turned to anger. Having already realized that no matter how good I was, I would always be Fat, Stupid and Ugly, I no longer wanted to follow the rules. Still subjected to Arnold's nightly assaults, I started playing around with boys and drinking, quickly discovering that alcohol could numb the pain. I went to "chugalug" parties and drank "like a boy," pouring the beer right down my throat. It was at this time also that my lifelong war with Fat began in earnest.

Everyone in my family was small. Except me. My grandparents, parents and sisters were all constructed on a smaller scale, and by the time I had reached my full height at age thirteen, I towered over everyone. So I was not only fat, but I was also this big Thing. Only Minnie could make me feel small. When she scooped me up in her soft, bosomy embrace, I'd immediately know that I was not a giant; I was just Debbie.

Over meals, Fat Stupid Ugly was reiterated a million ways, a million times. Arnold would scream at me. Mother would make pancakes and say eat, eat. Then, when I ate, she'd say, "How can you eat so much? It makes you fat."

Although a day didn't go by without a reminder of my size, one day my fatness reached a critical juncture. I remember trying on my new pink one-piece bathing suit when Arnold reacted with disgust. Mother didn't dispute his opinion; she took me to a diet doctor. I was twelve.

The doctor prescribed Preludin. It must have had some effect because I remember my grandfather later commenting on my "chicken legs," but I never felt any thinner. The real impact of the pills was on my sleep. Preludin is a stimulant, and I was wired day and night. To get to sleep, I stole Mother's phenobarbital. Thus began an upper-downer habit that would stay with me until I was in my twenties.

Wired, angry and rebellious, at thirteen I would dress in my short-shorts, halter-top and high heels and walk up and down Great Neck Highway, distracting truck drivers. Rejecting the more appropriate neighborhood boys, I managed to find and date a seventeen-year-old named Pete, who became my willing accomplice in beer drinking, cigarette smoking and sex.

When I was fourteen, Nan and Arnold divorced. Mother finally acknowledged that Arnold had been disrespectful to both of us. Though there was never any discussion of his sexual predation on me, his rages had continued, visible and unchecked. What's more, he had become a notorious skirt-chaser. Mother packed up Wendy, Victoria and me and moved us to Milwaukee so we could be near Frances and Irving.

School in Milwaukee was no better than school in Long Island.

My new friends were the juvenile delinquents—the kids who cut classes, wore leather jackets, rode motorcycles and smoked cigarettes on the corner. I stood on the corner with them after school and loved riding on their bikes. They didn't care about my grades, never seemed to find me excessively fat or ugly and always welcomed me into their midst—especially because I brought my own cigarettes. My boyfriends and my future husband, Tony, were part of that crowd. None of us had a place among the cheerleaders, the jocks or the smart kids. If they were misfits, so was I.

Free of Arnold, I was more mixed up than ever. Nothing was right. I hated my father, and I was glad he was gone, but I *still* wanted his approval. Mad about everything that had happened, I was acting out and always fighting with Mother. She disapproved of everything I did and had absolutely no control over me. I couldn't stand being in the house with her. I loved my sisters and was in awe of their beauty and creativity, but my adolescence—and my years of abuse—had already made me "old" while they were still children. My grandparents, who might have provided me some respite, had moved to California to be closer to Irving's brothers. It was a terrible time.

There was one bright moment, when a really nice boy, Danny, asked me to the prom. He was a senior, the son of one of Mother's friends; I was in the eleventh grade. I got all dressed up, and the two of us double-dated with my good friend Susie and her boyfriend. We went to a pre-prom party; I drank way too much, passed out in the back seat of the car and never made it to the prom. This only confirmed Mother's anger and stepped up the fury that raged in our house.

Mother saw trouble brewing. My latest boyfriend, Tony, was a notorious bad boy, and Nan tried everything to keep us apart, including taking out a restraining order and even sleeping on the floor outside my bedroom door to keep me from sneaking out during the night. When that didn't work, she decided to send me away to "the Academy" in Illinois.

I should have been in the twelfth grade, but Academy policy was not to accept new students in their senior year, and my grades were terrible, so they made me repeat my junior year. I always thought of the place as reform school because they locked us in at night, but it did get Tony out of my life temporarily, and for a while I dated a nice, clean-cut boy.

Nevertheless, I managed, with my roommate's eager collusion, to sneak out of my first-floor bedroom window at 2 A.M., make footprints in the snow, climb back in, and then pull the alarm, hoping the housemother would be tricked into thinking a burglar was there. On other occasions, I called the housemother vile names for refusing to give my friends medicine when they were sick, and each week, after signing out to go to Sunday church services, I would escape with my roommate, Sherry, to pick up boys in bars in the nearby town.

If there was an up-side to the Academy experience, it was learning to cut hair. Sherry wanted to be a hairdresser and taught me all her tricks, so soon I was cutting and styling hair for anyone who would sit still long enough. If it hadn't been for typing, which proved to be a more lucrative skill, I probably would have ended up as a professional hairdresser. It's something I still enjoy.

Nan had divorced Arnold and sent me off to a different state, but she couldn't erase the confusion, pain and anger that burned through every thought I had about my father. He had hurt me beyond repair. I wanted him dead. So I "killed" him. One Saturday morning, I put on my best black clothes and announced to everyone that my father had died. I went into mourning and whipped up a storm of tears. But when the school administrator called Mother to express the Academy's deepest sorrow, Nan discounted the story; she wasn't amused. She was furious and so was the school.

The Academy had had enough of me and sent Nan a letter explaining that they would not be welcoming me back the following year. That ended my academic career. I didn't finish eleventh grade and never graduated from high school. Reading is still a challenge.

WORK, PART ONE

By the time I had reached the end of my bleak tenure as a student, I had already discovered that work offered me an entirely different look at the world. Instead of being ridiculed and punished, I was appreciated. Instead of being useless and stupid, I found that I had skills that were valued.

My best skill and, along with sewing, the only lasting achievement of my high school years, was typing. After two years of typing classes on crotchety old manual typewriters, I blazed along at eighty words a minute. Miraculously, even if I couldn't read well, I could type like crazy.

Once my grandparents moved to California, I spent my summers there. My uncle, David Mirisch, president of Braverman and Mirisch, a Hollywood advertising and public relations agency, was always able to find something for me to do. I answered phones and typed, summer after summer, watching the parade of stars pass through his office.

Grandpa Irving's business was supplying candy and popcorn to movie theaters. His three brothers, Harold, Walter, and Marvin Mirisch, had a movie production business, Monogram Pictures (later Allied Artists, then moving to United Artists). As hugely successful independent producers, they were responsible for some of the biggest hits of the 1960s, including *The Magnificent Seven*, *West Side Story*, *The Pink Panther*, and *In the Heat of the Night*.

Grandpa Irving took me to the studio or onto location, where I got to meet the movie stars and watch the filming of *Some Like It Hot*, *The Great Escape*, and *The Apartment*, among others. We'd also go to Uncle Harold and Aunt Lottie's house. In the living room, all the seats turned around, the artwork lifted up, a screen came down, the lights dimmed and we would get to see the newest movies as the butler served us ice cream sundaes.

Back home in Milwaukee at age seventeen, I went to work at Bob's Big Boy. That didn't last long. I was a lousy waitress, never able to get the orders right; when I yelled orders in to the cooks, the cooks yelled right back at me. The place was a hangout for high school students and a constant reminder of my bad old school days. At the end of each day, Tony would pick me up from work and grab all my tips to see which of the nickels and dimes loading down my pockets would fit into his coin collection.

After waitressing, I worked accounts receivable at a

hotel. How I got that job, I'll never know; numbers weren't exactly my strong suit. Then I was receptionist/secretary for a couple of elderly attorneys, and then secretaried for an architecture firm that was designing drapery for the opera in New York City.

My favorite job in Milwaukee was working for a sportswear manufacturer. I started as a general office clerk and moved on to efficiency expert, timing piecework: how long it took to insert a zipper or sew on a button. (I still run my life—and anyone else's if they allow me—by the clock. I time everyone and everything.) After that, I became a pattern model—"Fat Debbie" was a perfect size 9—and then an assistant trim buyer, a job I loved. I remember spending days taking inventory in a warehouse full of trim.

Besides loving the fabrics and trim and actually learning something for a change, I was able to be out of the house for ten to twelve hours a day. There never seemed to be any end to the work that needed doing, and although they paid me overtime, the money was less of an incentive than avoiding Tony, who was now my husband.

HUSBAND NUMBER ONE

When I was seventeen, Mother married Mel, and I married Tony. In spite of all of Nan's efforts, Tony and I had resumed seeing each other on the sly after I returned from the Academy. We were hanging out with a pretty tough crowd. I loved those kids; they loved me. No judgments. My best friend, sweet, gentle Ellie, was the daughter of a prostitute. (Years later, when Ellie was working in Las Vegas as a showgirl, she tracked me down. She wanted me to know that she had named her new baby girl, Debbie, after me. Not long after her call, Ellie committed suicide, a loss that is still poignant all these years later.)

Before I met him, Tony had cracked his head in a drunken wreck when he rammed his car into someone's house, right into their living room. Everyone blamed his erratic behavior on that accident, but before we got married he never laid a hand on me. One time I fell and chipped a tooth and Mother blamed Tony, but it wasn't his doing.

In spite of appearances, our relationship was pretty innocent. Frankly, after what I had been through, sex wasn't particularly alluring. But Mother and Mel were convinced otherwise, and one day it came to blows. They started yelling at me, "If you're going to *sleep* with him, why don't you *marry* him?" My denials fell on deaf ears. We fought and pulled at each other's hair. It was ugly. I stormed out of the house and don't remember where I went that night. I didn't *want* to marry Tony, but I decided *okay, you think I should marry him, I will!* We got a license—Mother signed for me—and wearing a green linen suit and a Jackie Kennedy–style pillbox hat, I went to the Milwaukee courthouse and became Mrs. Tony.

Our honeymoon was a day at the racetrack.

Wedded bliss was short-lived. Tony was a mean and habitual drunk. He had a beer threshold that worked like a light switch. He'd drink a certain number of beers, and suddenly one eye would close, and his personality would transform from easy-going to psychotic. Then he'd start battering me.

He'd punch me and smash me up against the wall and scream at me and beat me until I was black and blue. Day after day. He'd hit me until I was unconscious. He'd rip my clothes off and rape me. One time he tore off my clothes and I ran outside into the snow and hid naked under his car. He'd make me walk on glass while he read the bible to me. One day he killed my dog, a beautiful collie named Lady. I loved that dog—too much for Tony's taste. In a jealous rage, Tony threw her out the window of our third-floor apartment.

I would huddle myself into a corner, trying to be invisible. But Tony persisted in his violence, and I always had a black eye and bruises and bandages and slings—and a quick excuse. I slipped, I fell, I ran into a door.

Six months after we got married, I got pregnant. I knew that if I lived through the pregnancy, Tony would hurt our baby. I wanted an abortion. Satisfied at having married me off and busy with her own new husband, Mother hadn't been around much during this time, but I called her, and she came through when I needed her most. She picked me up in the outskirts of Milwaukee and drove me downtown. We went into a desolate-looking building and found the office, where the doctor had his instruments in a turkey-roasting pan. He had me bite on a leather strap and close my eyes. Of course I couldn't tell Tony I had had an abortion, so I pretended that I had my period and survived another night.

Unfortunately, the abortion didn't bring me any closer to Mother, but after seeing me with a black eye, Wendy was concerned and parked herself in our apartment one day to protect me. Like Arnold, Tony had his public side and his private side. Nothing happened while Wendy was there, but once she left, Tony resumed his abuse.

I loved Tony's family. We lived with his parents for a while, and I took care of his mother when she was horribly ill with cancer. His violence wasn't just directed at me;

his parents were terrified of him, too. I remember finding his mother cowering at the bottom of the laundry chute. The police would come and handcuff Tony now and then, but somehow, he'd always be back, seething and explosive.

I don't know where I went when Tony started pounding on me, but I separated my mind from my body and just floated around somewhere else until it was over—or until one or the other of us passed out. One night when he was passed out, I took Tony's gun and held it to his head. I stood there for the longest time, wanting to kill him. But I saw him as so big and powerful that I was afraid that a little thing like a bullet wouldn't hurt him. He would only wake up and go crazy, and probably kill me instead.

After my cat disappeared mysteriously, I finally realized that to survive I had to leave and, over a number of weeks, cautiously crafted my plans. Tony's brother was a warm, intelligent man who knew how crazy Tony was. I called to warn him that I was going; I was afraid that Tony might hurt his parents when I left. Then, plans in place, I hastily packed a suitcase in the attic of his mother's house, called a friend for a ride to the airport, and flew to Los Angeles.

Within two days Tony was in L.A., but Grandpa and Uncle David had him arrested and taken back to the airport to fly home. He may have spent some time locked up after that, but he stayed obsessed. Nearly fifteen years later, Tony tracked down Nan and Mel and, through them, found me. He showed up at my door and tried to explain that he was different, that he had been "born again." Always willing to believe in the underdog, I let him stay with me for a couple of weeks until he began obsessively buying me presents and writing me poems. I became increasingly terrified and finally a couple of my friends coerced him into a car and drove him to the airport. I never heard from Tony again.

Arnold had readied me for a life of abuse, but after two and a half years with Tony, Arnold was looking more and more like a prince. That there might be a pattern or any deeper psychological implication to my marrying an abuser, never occurred to me. Worse than anything Tony could do to me physically was his repeated threat to injure my beautiful baby sister Victoria. Even from the distance of forty years, it seems like a miracle that he didn't hurt anyone in my family— and that he didn't kill me.

CALIFORNIA

Throughout my childhood, I was vaguely aware of Nan talking about her mother. The family called her Frantic Frances and whispered about her manic behavior, her suicide attempts, her shock treatments and her years of therapy. But this was my dear little Grandma Frances who sent me exquisite dolls from her travels, gave me beautiful clothes out of her closet and sheltered me from my father's brutality. If she was dramatic or troubled or burdened with unhappiness, she didn't share it with me, and I loved her dearly.

As I secretly planned my escape from Tony, I was certain of only one thing: I would live with Frances and Irving in California. I bought my plane ticket, and a month before I planned to leave, I placed a person-to-person call to Grandpa. I would explain my plans to him, including all the details about my flights and arrival, and let *him* tell Grandma Frances. I was terrified of Tony, but I was also very excited about the idea of living with my grand-parents, and I knew that Grandma would be very emo-tional and excited, too. I was concerned that she might get overwrought—losing sleep, launching herself into a frenzy of activity, shopping and returning things, redeco-rating my room and making everything perfect for me. I wanted Grandpa, who was always very calm, to be with her when she found out I was coming.

The operator placed the call, and Grandma answered the phone. I heard her voice and then the operator's voice asking for Grandpa and then Grandma saying that he wasn't home. I told the operator I would try again later.

Just a few hours after my call, Grandpa Irving found Grandma Frances dead. She had hanged herself in her closet. It was horrible. I could picture her there, sur-rounded by her soft, silky clothes. It was one of the most devastating experiences of my life, compounding the abuse by Arnold and Tony, and leaving me with twenty years of guilt and regret. It was further proof that I couldn't do anything right, that I was Stupid. Even after I learned that Grandma Frances had made her plans ahead of time—buying a rope and giving the household help the day off—I was certain that if only I had spoken with her that morning, Grandma would still be alive.

As shaken as I was by Grandma's suicide, I had to get away from Tony. Living in California wouldn't be the same without her, but my plans were in motion, and I knew that Grandpa would protect me. I moved in with Grandpa Irving, and we both attempted to recover from our loss. Though we had never been terribly close—my greatest affection had been lavished on Grandma Frances—Grandpa had always been kind to me. Once I moved to California, we grew closer. I was only nineteen, emotionally scarred and deeply troubled, but my survival had depended on my ability to conceal my pain, and I did everything I could to lead a "normal" life.

I went back to work for Uncle David, settling in where I had left off during my summers in California. But now I was older and quickly picked up the tools of the trade, learning skills that I've valued ever since. I learned how to write ads and press releases and deal with the media. I got an inside look at the movie industry, talked with movie stars and reporters at the daily papers and the trades, made friends and worked with some very talented people. I even found a place on the job for my haircutting skills, trimming and styling my uncle's business partner's hair before she appeared at big meetings.

I drove to work in my 1964 Mini Cooper. It had been refitted in a Rolls-Royce factory and had starred as the get-away car in the Peter Sellers Pink Panther movie *A Shot in the Dark.* Grandpa Irving had bought it from his brother, Uncle Harold, for a dollar. It had electric windows that wouldn't open in the heat and windshield wipers that wouldn't work in the rain, and once, going over a bump, the radiator burst. But aside from that, it had a beautiful leather and walnut interior and wicker-patterned sides, and I even managed to get a speeding ticket going eighty miles an hour down Wilshire Boulevard in heavy traffic.

The cop said he just saw the antenna go by.

After a while, I left my job and was hired as a management trainee at Gemco, a huge membership department store. I was the first woman and the first non-college graduate in the training program. I was made manager of children's clothing for the brand new Glendora store, my first experience managing other people, and then was promoted to warehouse foreman, supervising a large crew of unskilled workers who priced and packed goods going to all the other stores.

Over the next few years, I worked in the reservation office at a hotel, was a grocery checker, typed transcripts of press interviews, worked hospital security and employee health services, and did piecework as a seamstress, sewing wedding dresses and leather vests. I thought about becoming a court reporter or a nurse, but those were out of the question without a high school diploma.

I did a lot of sewing and decided I wanted to work in the motion picture business designing costumes. Grandpa offered to pay for me to go to school to learn pattern making, so I signed up for classes at Santa Monica College. I was *so* proud. College! I wouldn't have to be a high school dropout for the rest of my life.

I showed up that first day for my pattern-making class, and I couldn't have been any more excited. I sat down in the classroom and looked around, surprised to see that all of the other students were young men. There were no sewing machines, just big tables and huge pieces of industrial equipment. It turned out to be a class on making patterns for machinery. The first things we made were a nut and a bolt. I stuck with it until one of the boys bloodied himself on a saw. I never told Grandpa I had quit. I just kept working.

As it would for many years to come, work allowed me to conceal my pain. At work, I could be productive and cheerful and competent. But in my hours away from the office, I would sit in my apartment, endlessly staring at nothing, not watching television, not talking to anyone, not moving from my chair. I had so successfully separated my living self from the pain of the abuse by Arnold and Tony, and the loss of Grandma, that I was emotionally dead.

After living with Grandpa Irving for a year, I found an apartment in Beverly Glen Canyon, where my red closet became my secret hideaway. Instead of sitting in a corner, or hiding under the covers or staring at a wall, I had a truly safe place of my own. I could close the door, shut out the noisy, frightening world around me and retreat into the darkened silence of my disturbed and damaged mind.

About that time, Nan, Mel, Wendy and Victoria moved to California. Now that she was living nearby (and safe from Tony's threats), Victoria could spend weekends with me in my tiny apartment. One of my friends remembers coming over and finding her sound asleep in a heap of blankets in the bathtub. One weekend when she was eleven or twelve, Vic visited me in my basement apartment on Chrysanthemum Lane. It rained, and then it rained some more, and then it poured, and then my car floated down the hill and got tangled in the bushes. The roads were closed, and we were stuck without anything to eat, so we ordered pizza and, unbelievably, it showed up at our door. We loved being sisters—and friends.

Another very important development in my life around that time was Dr. Raymond. In spite of feeling that therapy had failed with Grandma Frances, Grandpa Irving knew that I needed help and found a doctor who could provide it.

Three days a week for over three years, I took my shattered Humpty Dumpty self to Dr. Raymond's office and he slowly helped me find the glue to piece myself back together. As he helped me cope with the challenges of daily living, Dr. Raymond also helped me begin, slowly and painfully, to explore my emotions. I began to *feel*, and my long-hidden feelings frightened me. I would see Dr. Raymond on Monday and by Tuesday I would feel as if a week had passed since our last meeting; after our Wednesday session, Thursday would be pure hell. In between I would call him again and again, terrified. I would go to a movie and be so scared that I would take my high heels off and run miles back to my apartment, barefoot, to hide in the closet. My demons were everywhere.

One of my demons was the little "fat" pill I had been taking since I was twelve. Now in my twenties and desperately addicted to Preludin, I would tell any lie to get it. When I showed up at Dr. Raymond's office with a

103-degree fever and a painful kidney infection, he gently questioned me, discovered that I had diet and sleep prescriptions from several different doctors, sorted everything out and at last helped me to quit taking diet pills. My fight against Fat continued unabated—now unaided by my trusty pills.

My closest companion was my huge, sweet, gentle dog, Elphants. He was a mutt, the size of a small horse and covered with wild-looking hair. When I took him to Beverly Glen Park, children would rush over excitedly and beg for rides, clamber up onto his back one at a time and clutch onto his fur as he patiently walked them across the grass. But away from the park, people would cross to the other side of the street when they saw us coming, which was just fine with me. I borrowed his power and pretended to be in control.

One day, some months into my therapy, I was walking down Sunset Boulevard with Elphants when this young man came up and started talking to me. His said his name was Sandy. He wasn't afraid of Elphants. He was a painter, carrying an easel, and he told me that he had just been released from prison and had no place to live. He seemed gentle and friendly. I sympathized with his situation, and Elphants liked him. I told him he could come home with me, and he did. He slept in the bed; I slept in the closet. He was kind to me and often called Dr. Raymond to try to help. We were friends and, after a long time and without much fuss, lovers, moving together to another house in Beverly Glen Canyon where he had an art studio. But it was almost as if we lived in separate worlds. One afternoon I walked into the apartment and there was Sandy, shooting up. I guess he was always shooting up, I had just never noticed. It was my hard-won healing with Dr. Raymond that had opened my eyes.

During Arnold's, and then Tony's, abuse, I had protected myself by shutting down my senses. If I couldn't *feel*, they couldn't hurt me. At work I was safe, but away from the structure of an office, I was assaulted by the intensity of the world around me. Anything could terrify me—a movie, loud music, people yelling, an adult hitting a child—and make me feel that I would shatter into a million pieces. It was safer not to see.

With great patience, Dr. Raymond helped me build on my small successes—my competence at work, my sewing, my loving relationships with my sisters—and begin to see beyond my internal world. His dedication started to show results. My ability to have a physical relationship with Sandy was one sign that I was healing; new friendships with my neighbors in the Canyon was another.

One day I realized that I was seeing colors—that for years, since Tony, I had lived in a black and gray world, and now everything was changed. When I hear the words "born again," that's the feeling that comes to mind. I walked around dazzled by the flowers, the trees, the textures and colors of the world around me. Everyone thought I was tripping on LSD, but I wasn't. I was *seeing*. And feeling.

After three years of therapy, we agreed that it was time

for me to "graduate." I still felt fragile and not entirely sure of my ability to function without Dr. Raymond's constant support. But I understood that my confidence and strength would slowly increase as I tested myself—on my own, in the real world.

Dr. Raymond was a healer. He helped me take the first step out of my closet and probably saved my life. He helped me see that in spite of my painful past, I could have a meaningful present and future. Remarkably, we never once discussed the sexual abuse that I had experienced at the hands of my father. Dr. Raymond knew I wasn't ready.

HUSBAND NUMBER TWO

Except for a couple of visits to New York after Nan and Arnold divorced, I never saw my father again. He had two wives after Nan, and a son, whom I've never met. In 1970, at age forty-eight, Arnold died of a massive coronary. I was twenty-three. With a bitter and confused mixture of love and hate, I had pretended that he was dead when I was at the Academy, but that didn't prepare me for the actual event. When I found out that he was really dead, I cut myself, broke his paintings in half and ripped apart my apartment in a blaze of anger. I just wanted to go back *one time* and have him tell me that I was really okay: that I wasn't fat, stupid, and ugly. Now I had to face the reality: it would never happen.

Still, I was moving along in my life. Working, as always. Dating. Living in one apartment or another in Beverly Glen Canyon. I had friends and dogs and a cat named Kabir. Elphants had stayed with Sandy after we broke up, and I now had Charlie, a chow, and Bubbala, my all-time dog of dogs. Bub was a fifteen-pound wire-haired terrier sort of dog who never would have won any beauty contests. I remember pulling into a gas station and the attendant saying, "Oh my god, was that dog in a fire?" Bub slept with me, went to work with me, and once, when I was delirious with a high fever, I saw Bub dressed as a nurse, taking care of me.

I met Steve through one of my friends. He drove a former UPS truck, and I drove a British Commer Imp van that I had outfitted with a bed and shelves. (It had great character but terrible brakes. I would have to stop repeatedly to put in brake fluid, and if Charlie or Bub saw anything interesting while I was stopped, they would jump out and give chase, and then I gave chase after them—a whole lot of effort for a little brake fluid.) Steve was in the family fabric business, and on one of our first dates, we installed draperies in a mutual friend's apartment.

We went out for a while, and then we broke up, and I went out with Steve's roommate. He became my fiancé until late one night he rushed into my apartment, waking me as he yelled and jerked the blanket off of me as I lay in bed. Something I had said to him on the phone had made him jealous and angry. He didn't hit me, and he had never hurt me or been violent before, but his actions triggered a flood of horrible memories. In my nightgown, I ran to my car, threw the dogs in and raced off at top speed as he was clinging to my rear bumper.

I resumed dating Steve, and eventually we started living

together. We shared creative interests and, working together, seemed able to accomplish a great deal. Through a mutual friend, I met a man who did tapestry work on huge wall hangings. I was intrigued and asked him to teach me how to weave. He showed me some simple techniques, and I did my first weaving on threads stretched between two branches. I *loved* weaving—the variations in the yarns and being able to create something quickly that I could see and touch. It's an artistic passion that continues to the present day. That first piece still hangs on the wall in Mother's house.

Grandpa Irving liked Steve a lot. Every time he talked to me, he'd call me "Mrs. Steve." We had invited Grandpa to have brunch with us one Sunday morning and were waiting for him when Mother called to say that Grandpa Irving had died. I was terribly sad. It had been less than a year since my father had died and just a few years since Grandma Frances' shocking death. Grandpa had been my staunch supporter: accepting, generous and kind, without judgment. He was an anchor in my storm-tossed life. Now he was gone.

Steve was serious and sympathetic as I processed this new loss. He seemed perfect to me: gentle, tall, not one bit volatile, and he would never, *ever* lay a hand on me. He valued work, as I did, and found a place in his life for creativity. I saw in him the father for the child I had always wanted. So we got married. That was 1971.

We had a hippie wedding in Mother's backyard. We were both from Jewish families, but neither of us was religious, so we found a minister to preside at the ceremony. My sister Victoria played the guitar and sang folk songs. I wore a long purple dress and almost passed out from excitement. Champagne flowed from a fountain. The whole family participated, my current boss from the hospital was there, and it was a really wonderful day. We went to Big Sur and stayed in the honeymoon suite at the Big Sur Inn, but we got homesick for our dogs and after two days headed back to Los Angeles.

We bought a house in Venice, California, and began to fix it up. It was fun and satisfying. We both had a feeling for design and could always see the potential in a house, if it had any. Show me a dump, and I see a mansion.

Four months after we got married, I got pregnant. I had been to the Venice Family Clinic, and when I came out I grabbed Bub out of the car, threw him into the air and screamed with delight, "Bub, I'm pregnant!"

I *loved* being pregnant. I could have stayed pregnant for a few years. I wore my long, flowing, bedspread-fabric hippie dresses and walked along the Venice beach talking to my baby-to-be, barefoot and very happy.

Steve and I had lots of cars, including a series of Morris Minors. We each had one, and we kept one for parts. We had convertibles, hardtops and wagons. We repaired our cars together, and when I was eight months pregnant, Steve taught me how to do a valve job. His mother came over to the house one day and asked Steve where I was. He pulled me out from under the car.

We went to Lamaze training. I decided that I had to

have my baby at home, and we found a doctor who would do a home delivery. The fact that he was beyond retirement age and lived at the other end of the county didn't seem to matter at first, but when I got a bad ear infection in my eighth month, Steve became increasingly anxious that I would die, the baby would die, or that he'd have to deliver the baby himself. Lamaze or no Lamaze, he wasn't ready for that. Steve insisted that I give birth in the nearby hospital, and I agreed, with the stipulation that I would come home immediately afterward.

So about 10 P.M. on May 21, I told Steve that I thought I was in labor. He was oblivious, totally engrossed in a movie on TV until his mother called. I told her what was going on, and she instructed him to take me to the hospital immediately. We arrived at midnight, and I went into hard labor at around 2 A.M. I ran around the room doing my breathing, jumped onto the table and at 4:30 A.M. on May 22, 1972, Gideon was born. I watched him coming out of me, and I saw his perfect little nails that looked just like Steve's nails, and the first words out of my mouth were, "I can't live without doing this again." I nursed him instantly, and then they took him away and stitched me up. Already anxious at his absence, I tugged my feet out of the stirrup straps, leaped off the table and went looking for my baby. I wouldn't take my eyes off of him for a second. Handing me precious little baby gifts, Mother was hiding under the bed, so they wouldn't kick her out of the hospital. We all went home by 9 A.M.

If ever there was a child that was wanted, it was Gideon.

I had wanted a child all my life. I had practiced on my dolls, but I had dreamed of a real baby. I was ecstatic through my pregnancy and couldn't imagine being a mother to anyone more perfect and beautiful than this little boy. And I knew exactly what to do: I treated him the way I treated my dolls, loving him more than anything in the world. I nursed him, fed him, changed him and sewed for him. I didn't hit him or molest him or call him names. He was my living doll.

I had fulfilled my one lifetime dream—to become a mother—and I was as happy as I could possibly be. When Steve was transferred to Seattle, we moved to the Northwest. In our spare time, we restored old houses, buying and selling them along with the antiques that we had collected. Steve did stained glass, and I returned to my weaving. It was a creative and artistic time. Yet, I began to feel a stirring of discontent. I needed expressions of love and affection that were missing from my marriage.

Steve and I kept moving. We'd buy a house, upgrade the kitchen, lay new floors, paint it inside and out, maybe put up some wallpaper and, just about the time the house was really comfortable, we'd find another one. So we'd start over again. Tudor, country style, colonial—it didn't matter. We both liked doing the work and seeing the results.

Gideon never had a chance to cry. The second he made a peep, I'd pick him up and hold him or nurse him. Mother kept saying, why don't you wean him, you're going to be nursing him when he's in college. And I'd say, quit saying that, he'll nurse until he stops and that's the way it's going to be. And that's the way it was. Until he was three, the only words that Gideon spoke were, "Wean it, Mom." He figured out that his grandmother's word had something to do with being held and nursed. We would be walking through the market, and all of a sudden I would hear, "Wean it, Mom."

That he didn't say anything else did not worry me. He smiled and laughed all the time, understood what was said to him and responded appropriately. When he was ready to talk, he talked. I was on the phone with his best friend Jeremy's mother when Gideon picked up the extension and said, "Can I talk to Jeremy?" Jeremy heard about this and ran around the neighborhood screaming, "Gideon talked! Gideon talked!"

I found a huge, expensive floor loom that I wanted and decided to finance the cost with sewing. I designed a skirt made from used blue jeans and figured that I would be able to sell a few of them to pay for my loom. Much to my surprise, the first store I walked into placed an enormous order. Steve could always see the dollar signs in an idea, so instead of making a dozen skirts, we made hundreds. We turned our living room and dining room into a little factory, had a bunch of different designs and cranked out skirts day and night. We had three industrial sewing machines and a large pinning table, and I recruited some of my new friends and neighbors to sew with me. To get denim, we first went to the Salvation Army and picked through the used jeans. Then I found out that we could order used denim in 500-pound bales. A truck would pull up to the house and deposit these gigantic bales of denim on the sidewalk. We'd remove the strapping and haul the denim into the house by the armload. There I was, sewing, nursing Gideon. I loved what I was doing. But my original goal had been to purchase the loom, so I sold the business to a couple down the block. I wanted to concentrate on weaving.

I bought the loom. It was a huge thing, nearly the size of a grand piano and just about as complicated. I didn't have a clue how to work it, but it gave me license to buy the most gorgeous fibers, and before long, I had moved the bed downstairs into the living room in order to use the upstairs bedroom for my loom, which sat surrounded by overflowing baskets of colorful wool, linen and cotton yarns.

Having failed to decipher the loom's printed instructions, I went in search of guidance. Through a small Seattle art college, The Factory of Visual Art, I found Judith, a weaving teacher who was willing to come to my house. Thereafter, week in and week out, she patiently tutored me in the language of warp and weft, heddle and shuttle.

Threading a large floor loom is an eye-crossing tangle to a dyslexic adult. Just preparing the yarn to go on the loom is a math problem. But Judith taught me, and remarkably, I learned. When I finished a tapestry I would cut the strings, roll it up, drive to her apartment and make her give me a grade on my weaving.

Within the confines of this very traditional medium, I discovered my creative passion for color, texture and design. Fingers flying, I turned out weaving after weaving, each one inspiring visions of the next . . . sailboats, lighthouses, city scenes, people, sheep . . . anything could turn into a tapestry. And once I had gained some control of the medium, I found that I could challenge it. I could weave *on* anything—frames and branches, driftwood and mirrors—and *with* anything—ribbon and raffia, leather and buttons, feathers and fur.

Beyond the sheer excitement of creating, I also discovered that my weavings had an audience. People wanted to buy my work. I did commissions and sold my weavings at craft stores and art fairs, sharing a booth with my dear friend Barb, a ceramic artist.

Steve was still working and doing stained glass, and the antiques would come and go. I'd finish a weaving, and he'd build a beautiful frame for it. We had a pair of antique barber chairs in the living room, and I became the neighborhood haircutter. I kept looking for a church pew that I could cut in half and use as a seat in our kitchen. Steve was out of town when I found a church that was selling its pews, but they wouldn't sell me just one, so I bought all of the pews, a pulpit and some stained glass windows. When Steve came home, we had a little church set up right there in our living room.

Finally, we made an offer on a huge estate behind our house in Seattle, but the offer was rejected, so we moved to Oakland.

Steve and I had been married five years. I now had what I had wanted more than anything in the world: a child. I had my weaving, my friends, and my work on the houses and the cars. But that was the external world. Since my therapy with Dr. Raymond, I had slowly emerged from my physical and psychological closet of defenses; instead of being completely shut down, I began to have *feelings* and was frightened by their untamed force. Inside, where my feelings churned, I was haunted by a familiar face: Fat Stupid Ugly Debbie.

Although I was no longer taking Preludin, I continued to diet compulsively. Still traumatized by my nightmarish childhood scenes at the dinner table, I was unable to sit down with my family or friends for a normal meal. I equated sitting at the table with punishment and abuse. I would "hover" during meals, cooking and serving, walking around fussing with plates and trays, making "important" phone calls and lingering in the kitchen. If my bottom ever touched a chair, it was only for a moment. I'd always bounce back up and find something else to do.

My persistent identity as Stupid and Ugly still took its toll. Although I shopped for groceries, antiques and yarn, I otherwise rarely left the house. My friends, neighbors and customers came to visit me. Gideon's friends came over and played with him at our house. The house was my closet.

After years of being grateful for Steve's gentleness and reserve, I felt increasingly hungry for intensity and passion, now seeing Steve as a roommate and business partner. Our relationship was about doing, not about feeling; I wanted somebody demonstrative. As horrible as my experiences with Arnold and Tony had been, they had been *intense*. I knew I didn't want the pain and violence, but I craved something more than the emotionally bland coolness of my marriage.

To protect myself from this confusing upwelling of feelings, I drank wine. I had stopped drinking entirely while I was pregnant, but now I found that a glass or two of wine took the edge off of my anxiety, doubts and desires. I didn't get drunk, and the wine didn't seem to interfere with my ability to weave, cook or be a mother to Gideon. It dulled my discontent, but not completely. I wanted out of the marriage.

Steve and I went to therapy for six months. In what turned out to be our final session, when I said wouldn't it be nice if sometime we held hands, Steve explained that he wasn't the kind of person who would ever want to do that. He wasn't ready for divorce, but strengthened by some therapy, my growing creativity and the first years of my dream-come-true motherhood, I was once again feeling as if life's rules didn't apply to me. So while it wasn't what Steve wanted, we decided to divorce.

Steve remarried, and over the years, we have stayed in contact; Steve and his wife have been kind to Gideon and to me.

If my marriage to Steve was the calm in the eye of the storm, the end of my marriage was followed by one of the most intense times of my already tumultuous life.

THE WILD YEARS

Separated from Steve, I learned that a lot of my old Beverly Glen Canyon friends had moved north and were now living in Berkeley, Oakland or San Francisco. I wanted laughter, passion and carefree fun—anything that could distract me from that Fat Stupid Ugly little girl living inside me. I quickly discovered that I had arrived in the right place at the right time.

Four-year-old Gideon in tow, I was without husband or work but surrounded by generous friends. There was a neighborly, supportive, open-door feeling among our various little families. We didn't live together, but it was almost as if we were part of a commune; there was always someone to watch after the children, pick up something at the store or cook a meal. Gideon made friends and was a bright, happy child.

Mac was the friend of a friend, very good looking, very sexy and very smart, with a wonderful dry sense of humor. He was a big drug dealer, and I fell madly in love with him. He had a college degree and was married with children but separated from his wife, so in some way I knew that he was "safe": he'd never be completely available to me. I loved the way he communicated with me; he listened, and he made me feel beautiful. He was very kind and loving, very political, always fighting for the underdog. Still is.

It was a time of easy money and fast friends. Years before, in Beverly Glen Canyon, when I had been working, my friends would sometimes be strapped for cash, and I would give them money without a second thought. Now they were there for me, giving me whatever I needed for rent or a car or Gideon's school. In exchange, I helped them with babysitting, bookkeeping and secretarial tasks. With their open-handed assistance, I managed to get by comfortably without holding a "regular" job.

Being with Mac was wild and always fun. It's not that he looked or acted wild; it was a slow undertow, a quiet wild. He was a pilot and had a plane and would fly to Mexico to make drug connections, sometimes taking me along. He would put the plane on autopilot, and we'd make love in the sky. It still wasn't easy for me to venture far from home; I was usually loaded on pot, booze, cocaine or all three. I was in love. I lost weight.

One time we flew to Mazatlan, and in a colorful market, Mac bought me a baby green parrot. We put Puff on a huge boat with bales of marijuana, and he headed north, munching marijuana seeds. We picked him up once he reached California, and he'd fly loose around my apartment, take showers with me and sit on my head while I washed the dishes. He squawked happily, and if he occasionally left splats of "guacamole" on the furniture, I'd wash that, too. A few years later, Gideon and I moved, with Puff, back to Los Angeles. A living reminder of my love affair with Mac, Puff was with us for a long time until one day Gideon walked into the kitchen, looking sad, and there was Puff: a little green pile of feathers lying still at the bottom of the cage.

So my friends were drug dealers. They knew how to dress up, eat well, travel in style and have a good time. They smoked some pot and drank champagne, but they weren't heavy dopers. They were students, parents, artists and businesspeople. And if sometimes I felt like a mob gal, I enjoyed this part of my life. There was risk and passion and adventure. And there were people who protected and cared deeply for one another and for me. I continued to see Mac on and off for years. He saw me through my highs and lows and back again, and I will always count him among my dearest friends.

In the midst of these wild times, I came up with the idea of bartending as the perfect job. I could be home with Gideon and do my weaving during the day, and work at night while Gideon slept, making decent money to support the two of us. So once again, I enrolled in school, this time at the Berkeley School of Bartending. Never did I imagine that memorizing hundreds of recipes would be so difficult. The reading and numbers were agonizing, but by this time I could talk to anyone, and I knew something about drinking, so I stuck with it.

Gideon must have just started reading, and every day he would test me with my three-by-five recipe cards. My friends took me out shopping, and I bought all these Lucille Ball–style bartending outfits—off-the-shoulder blouses, cinched waists, short, flouncy skirts. I went to school every day and studied really, really hard. I memorized my recipes and practiced making all kinds of exotic drinks, and finally, I graduated. My friends threw me a big party. I was very proud. It's the only diploma I've ever earned, and it's still framed and hanging on my wall.

One week later, I found out I had cancer.

CANCER

There had been a small cluster of symptoms. I had back pain similar to what you'd feel if you lifted something the wrong way. It came and went. But I also had intermittent bleeding.

At first, I didn't pay much attention to these minor inconveniences, but as they seemed to worsen, I mentioned it to one of my friends. She insisted that I see a doctor. So I went to a doctor and had my exam and everything came back normal. But the symptoms persisted, so I went to another doctor. Same thing: everything's normal. I even went to the emergency room in terrible pain. They told me not to worry—that I had "female problems." This happened several times: different doctors, different facilities, more symptoms, normal results.

Finally, my friends helped me find (and pay for) a doctor who would look beyond the simple tests. At our first appointment, Dr. Nishimine looked over all my test results and said he wanted to do a D&C (dilation and curettage). That should turn up the cause of the bleeding. So I had the D&C and it was normal. Nothing.

But my symptoms continued, and he wouldn't give up, so he decided to do some live biopsies. After Dr. N. took the tissue samples, Gideon and I flew to Los Angeles to visit Mother. There was no special occasion, just a family visit. But while we were sitting at the kitchen table talking, Dr. N. called and said, "We got the results of your biopsy. You have acute invasive cancer of the cervix and uterus." I was thirty.

He told me I had two choices: they could treat it with massive doses of radiation, which would probably burn out my vagina, so they would have to rebuild it later, or I could go to New York, where there was a specialist who could perform a Wertheim's hysterectomy.*

I flew back to Oakland and went to see Dr. N., and I told him no, that I *wasn't* going to have a burnt-out vagina, and I *wasn't* going to fly to New York for surgery. Those were not acceptable options. I told him *he* had to do the surgery, or I wasn't going to do anything at all. I told him to start studying; my life was in his hands.

Why he agreed to this, I don't know, but I had laid down my rules and offered myself up as a guinea pig, and he seemed up to the task. (He later went on to specialize in this procedure.)

Dr. N. wanted to schedule the surgery as soon as

---

*Also known as a radical hysterectomy, Wertheim's involves the surgical removal of one or both of the ovaries, the fallopian tubes, the cervix and the entire uterus, nearby lymph nodes, and part of the vagina.

possible; the cells were replicating and every day put me at greater risk. There was so much to do. My friends, all my drug-dealing Bay Area pals, were suddenly everywhere at once—helping me with Gideon, driving me around, bringing me presents and, of course, keeping me supplied with whatever I needed to numb the physical and psychological pain.

I wasn't working, my credit cards were maxed out and I didn't have money to pay for the surgery, so I had to apply for emergency Medi-Cal. I sat in the office with Gideon for hours and hours waiting for my paperwork to be processed. I spent days in the hospital undergoing one test after another, one X-ray after another, literally head to toe.

Three days before the surgery, Mother flew in to help me. We went shopping. I tried on dresses. The important thing was not that I had a life-threatening illness, but that I *looked* great: a perfect 113 pounds. Mother told me, for the first and only time, that my figure looked beautiful. I might not live, but at least I would die with a 24-inch waist. There are pictures of me from right before the surgery lying on my hospital bed, very tan, wearing a bikini, with a thin gold chain around my waist.

Mother and I managed to spend some loving time together in those three days. But in one of our conversations, I remember saying to Mother, please, if anything happens to me, and I don't survive this surgery, you have to make sure that Gideon is taken care of. She got a look of panic on her face and started pulling at her hair, screaming, "You *have* to stay. *You* have to take care of *me.*"

When I checked into the hospital, it was like an Irish wake. I always had a glass of wine in one hand, a cigarette in the other. I had my music playing, and my friends were with me all the time. My sister Victoria was there. Nan was there. All I really wanted was to see Mac, and he was there, too. One time we actually made love in the waiting room.

The night before the surgery was busy. I had been acting as a sort of secretary for my drug-dealing friends, and I knew where all the money was buried. Literally. Concerned that I might die and take the secret with me, a few of my pals showed up at the hospital and asked me to draw them a little treasure map. People were in and out at all hours. The wine flowed.

Gideon was going to stay with Steve while I was in the hospital. He was small and serious and worried. He had overheard enough adult conversations to understand that something frightening was about to happen. Steve brought him up to my room to say goodbye, and I held him and kissed him. Steve later told me that the minute my surgery started, Gideon passed out and stayed asleep until the surgery was over, six hours later. Only in retrospect did I see how traumatized he was. After my surgery, Gideon lost most of his hearing for nearly a year and had to repeat a year of school.

I said my good-byes, and they wheeled me out and spent the next six hours taking me apart and piecing me back together. All I remember was waking up asking for cigarettes, and then the doctors explaining that they were doing biopsies to see if I would need radiation. I went nuts. The whole reason I had had this radical surgery was to *avoid* the drastic radiation. I tried to get up, screaming and pulling out all the tubes that were stuck in me. If I had known that radiation was even a remote possibility, I never would have opted for the surgery.

I was in a lot of pain. They pumped me full of drugs, and I quieted down for a few days.

When I woke up again, there were flowers everywhere. My room looked like a mortuary. (To this day, I hate flowers in a hospital room.) The biopsies turned out fine. Once I was out of recovery, Mother went home. I was on intravenous everything, but always managed to have my wine. I had all these little wine bottles lined up in my bedside cabinet. I had my Paddington Bear in bed with me, and during Mac's many visits, he would join me under the covers, and we would watch *Casablanca*.

In a matter of hours, my childhood fantasy of sitting at the table surrounded by my six sons had been sliced up and removed from my body forever, leaving a sad emptiness in its place. As I was getting ready to leave, I had to step on a scale. I had gained two pounds, and I was furious. In between his visits with me, Mac had gotten back together with his wife, and I was upset about that. The nurses told me I had to have a catheter and a urine bag when I went home, and that pushed me over the edge. I said absolutely not, and once they saw I could pee normally they released me without it. It was May 22, 1978, Gideon's sixth birthday.

HUSBAND NUMBER THREE

Gideon quickly became adept at fending for himself—and for me. After the surgery, my friends generously offered me the use of their vacation house in the country for my recovery. It sounded ideal: Gideon and I would have some time alone to recover. Just as we were settling in, I fell down a flight of steps, reopening my surgical wounds. My little boy had to call for help. An emergency medical helicopter landed in a nearby field, picked us up and flew us back to the hospital in Oakland for treatment. Our country retreat came to an abrupt and painful end.

Within a fast couple of years, my life had yo-yoed me through dramatic ups and downs. I had left Steve, found the excitement and passion I craved and even gotten my bartending diploma. From there, it was a sickening plunge into cancer and surgery. I was well on my way to alcoholism, had a beautiful son, no work and my lover had just gotten back together with his wife. I did the obvious thing: I moved.

Los Angeles was familiar and safe. I had started over there once before, and I could do it again. I had discovered the allure of easy money and was selling a little hashish (supplied at no charge by my friends) to pay Gideon's Montessori tuition. I quickly found a job at a laser lightshow company, where my bosses seemed to have an unlimited supply of cocaine. Until I got too jumpy, I snorted a lot of coke. And whatever I was doing, my glass of wine was always full. But soon the ability to type anything and talk to anyone once again helped me find more reliable work, and I got a job assisting a Beverly Hills real estate agent—my first step into another new world.

Now without a father, Gideon would look longingly at Big Brother ads on television. He kept telling me he wanted a Big Brother. It seemed like a reasonable enough request, and I thought I might see if someone had a nice friend who would spend some time with my son. But I never quite managed to do anything about it.

I was planning a party for Gideon's seventh birthday— a trip to the roller rink with all his Montessori friends— and Gid kept saying, "I have to invite my friend Simon." I was vaguely aware that there was a neighbor in our building who had befriended my son. Every day when Gideon came home from school, Simon would be practicing soccer outside, and after getting acquainted, they had started to play soccer together. Gideon arranged for us to meet. Simon seemed very nice, and I invited him to the birthday party. Although he didn't know how to skate, he laced up his skates and went right out on the floor with the rest of us, anyway.

After that, Gideon took every opportunity to ask Simon over to our apartment. Simon was dark and attractive, a Sephardic Jew. He was a U.S. citizen but had been raised in Indonesia, and he would wear these sexy Indonesian sarongs. He was gentle and soft-spoken, but most important, he was crazy about Gideon and treated him with great respect.

Our visits became more regular. Simon took me to temple, was very romantic and seemed entirely different from anyone I had ever known. We fell in love. We were next-door neighbors, and while I always preferred the safety of my own home, Simon and Gideon moved freely back and forth between our two apartments. Finally, Gideon decided this had gone on long enough. He told Simon to marry me.

This was okay with Simon, and it was okay with me, and it was a dream come true for Gideon, but it was a horror for Simon's mother. I was not a practicing Jew, I was eight years older than her son and I had had radical surgery that would prevent me from giving her a grandchild. Simon's father was always very kind to me, but whenever we went to their house, Simon's mother would cook such spicy Indonesian food that I was convinced she was trying to poison me.

Gideon kept his goal in sight, and Simon and I got married. We were married in a synagogue by a rabbi. I wore an exquisite, long white gown with a train, and Gideon was the ring-bearer. My wild friends from Northern California all came in for the wedding and stayed in a swank hotel in Westwood, where Simon and I had booked a room for our wedding night.

After the reception, we went back to the hotel and Simon was ready to turn in, but I just wanted to party with my pals and their seemingly unlimited supply of Dom Pérignon and other intoxicants. I got loaded and confused. I wanted to be with my friends, not in the room with Simon. High on cocaine, I took off my high heels and walked barefoot through Westwood in my wedding dress, crying my eyes out, but eventually returning to the room and my new husband. We left the next day for a real honeymoon: two weeks in Hawaii.

When we came home, we gave up our West L.A. apartments and moved into Simon's house in Woodland Hills, in the San Fernando Valley. It was very suburban. Every day, Gideon and I would climb into my Subaru Brat, and I would drive up through Topanga Canyon, drop Gideon off at Santa Monica Montessori and continue on into Beverly Hills to work. At the end of the day, we'd repeat the trip in reverse.

Not too long after our wedding, Simon's parents took a trip out of the country and, without asking, left their frightened new Indonesian housekeeper to stay at our house. She spoke an exotic dialect that only Simon could understand and insisted on sleeping in a corner on the floor. At the grocery store, she would test the fruits and vegetables by biting into them. I felt horrible. Although she was older than I was, she seemed like an abused, abandoned child, dropped into a world that didn't make any sense to her, with people she didn't know. I wanted to help her but didn't know how. In some way, she reminded me of myself. When Simon's parents returned, she went back to their house, but eventually she ran away.

I began to think that she had the right idea. I had continued drinking, and Simon was smoking a lot of pot. Our ability to communicate collapsed. To top it off, Woodland Hills was hot. Not just hot, but like an oven. The house never cooled down, and in the evening, we would watch television in the backyard. I was always burning up. I couldn't sleep. After six months of marriage, I told Simon I was going to move. I packed, called the moving company, and left within twenty-four hours.

Gideon and I moved back to the Westside, where it was twenty degrees cooler. That was the formal end of the marriage, but we stayed very close, and Simon has remained a wonderful, hands-on stepfather to Gideon. I think they truly consider each other father and son.

Gideon got the big brother he wanted, and I continued doing what I did best: working and drinking.

WORK, PART TWO

lthough there were a few times over the years that I got by without working, and a number of times when my work was unconventional, work was never something I resented or tried to avoid. In fact, work was the place where I could momentarily forget the Stupid label that I had worn since childhood. I was never afraid of leaving one job and finding another. I knew that I could start at the bottom of any job and type my way to the top.

For most of the next fifteen years, with assorted interruptions, I worked in the real estate industry. I started out assisting individual agents and developers, learning to navigate the cutthroat world of Los Angeles Westside real estate.

A friend sent me to see Joyce Rey, even then one of the top agents in the country. I walked into her office for my interview. All the phones were ringing, so I did what seemed sensible: I started answering them. Joyce rushed past, told me to come with her, and we drove to Dino De Laurentiis's estate, where she was dropping off some papers. She hired me on the spot as her assistant.

The competition was fierce, and the rewards were potentially huge. An agent's ability to attract sellers and buyers had a direct impact on his or her income. I discovered that I was good at creating advertising that would draw attention and sell properties. Before long, instead of working for a single agent, I was working for a company. I found myself supervising advertising and public relations departments and overseeing multi-million-dollar budgets. The mansions of Beverly Hills, Bel Air and Hollywood became the raw material for marketing campaigns that would attract the movie stars and foreign princes who could afford to buy them.

While work was my respite from my personal anxieties, from time to time, on the way to lunch or a meeting, I'd catch my reflection in a window and see Arnold looking back at me. Here I was—like him, an advertising executive, hair cut short, a smoker, a drinker—emulating the father who had abused me. If there was irony in that, I managed to lessen its sting with another glass of wine.

Sometimes a few of us from the office would go out after work. We'd have drinks in a nearby fancy Chinese restaurant, and from the happy-hour buffet I would fill up an inter-office envelope with chicken wings for Gideon's dinner. Then I'd get in the car and collect Gideon from school. I was frequently loaded and usually

READER/CUSTOMER CARE SURVEY

We care about your opinions! Please take a moment to fill out our online Reader Survey at **http://survey.hcibooks.com**.
As a **"THANK YOU"** you will receive a **VALUABLE INSTANT COUPON** towards future book purchases
as well as a **SPECIAL GIFT** available only online! Or, you may mail this card back to us.

(PLEASE PRINT IN ALL CAPS)

First Name _____ MI. ____ Last Name _____

Address _____ City _____

State _____ Zip _____ Email _____

1. Gender
❏ Female   ❏ Male

2. Age
❏ 8 or younger
❏ 9-12   ❏ 13-16
❏ 17-20   ❏ 21-30
❏ 31+

3. Did you receive this book as a gift?
❏ Yes   ❏ No

4. Annual Household Income
❏ under $25,000
❏ $25,000 - $34,999
❏ $35,000 - $49,999
❏ $50,000 - $74,999
❏ over $75,000

5. What are the ages of the children living in your house?
❏ 0 - 14   ❏ 15+

6. Marital Status
❏ Single
❏ Married
❏ Divorced
❏ Widowed

7. How did you find out about the book?
(please choose one)
❏ Recommendation
❏ Store Display
❏ Online
❏ Catalog/Mailing
❏ Interview/Review

8. Where do you usually buy books?
(please choose one)
❏ Bookstore
❏ Online
❏ Book Club/Mail Order
❏ Price Club (Sam's Club, Costco's, etc.)
❏ Retail Store (Target, Wal-Mart, etc.)

9. What subject do you enjoy reading about the most?
(please choose one)
❏ Parenting/Family
❏ Relationships
❏ Recovery/Addictions
❏ Health/Nutrition
❏ Christianity
❏ Spirituality/Inspiration
❏ Business Self-help
❏ Women's Issues
❏ Sports

10. What attracts you most to a book?
(please choose one)
❏ Title
❏ Cover Design
❏ Author
❏ Content

TAPE IN MIDDLE; DO NOT STAPLE

BUSINESS REPLY MAIL
FIRST-CLASS MAIL PERMIT NO 45 DEERFIELD BEACH, FL

POSTAGE WILL BE PAID BY ADDRESSEE

Health Communications, Inc.
3201 SW 15th Street
Deerfield Beach FL 33442-9875

FOLD HERE

Comments

late. There were times when my vision was so blurred that I had to cover one eye. That I might be endangering my little boy, let alone other drivers, pedestrians or myself, never crossed my mind. (For a while, I had a Jeep Wrangler, and after I'd had a few glasses of wine, I'd make its tires squeal around the curves in a Beverly Hills parking garage or drive up onto the pristine front lawns of Beverly Hills estates, just to make Gideon laugh.)

In the early 1980s, there were two major independently owned real estate companies vying for the Westside market share. The competition stopped short of public name-calling, but not by much. I worked first for one, and then switched to the other, turning myself into a commodity in the competition and pushing my salary upward as I went.

People kept telling me that I should get my license— that I would be a great real estate agent and could make a lot more money than I'd ever make in advertising. I had an eye for the properties, the right personality, a flair for marketing and so many personal connections that it seemed like a great idea. My agent friends assured me that I'd have no trouble with the exams. Even people who weren't native English-speakers were able to pass these tests.

Committed and enthusiastic, I enrolled in real estate school. Three times. I signed up, paid the substantial tuition (once with a full "scholarship" from Wendy) and went to classes. For the first couple of weeks, I'd do fine. But gradually I'd find myself drowning in a chaotic swirl of numbers, words, keys and maps. It was a humiliating reminder of my school days, and it took three tries before I was willing to admit defeat.

If marriages, motherhood and work had previously helped me ignore many of the disturbing memories of my early abuse, it was now taking more and more wine to accomplish the task. I was once again in therapy, exposing the raw nerve ends of my past. Nobody ever told me I had a problem with drinking, least of all my therapist, Dr. A., who assured me that I could quit any time, just like I had quit smoking. Indeed I *had* quit smoking. For a day or two . . . now and then.

I can remember going over to Mother's house with Gideon on long, warm Southern California afternoons. I'd have my half-gallon of wine and lay out on a float in the pool, drinking myself into numbness. Then, as usual, I'd put Gideon in the car, and we'd drive home. No one ever suggested that I'd had enough, and it certainly never occurred to me. Everyone was aware of my troubled past and figured, so what if she has a few drinks?

I never put much emphasis on sports, music lessons or other activities for Gideon. Except for work and my few "safe" places, I was afraid of leaving the house and trusted that Gideon would somehow do what he wanted to do and learn what he needed to learn. (His sixth-grade teachers asked Gideon to tell me to stop "helping" him with his math homework; I was giving him wrong information.) My philosophy was Love—and making sure that he had toys, bikes, computers, anything and everything a child would want, before he asked for it, and always to share with his friends. I told him it doesn't matter if you're a garbage man, ditch digger, teacher or president; I just want you to be happy. When Gideon's teacher told me that Gideon was one of the few children that helped his disabled, injured or sad classmates, and that he thought like a leader, I could not possibly have been more proud. (Leader or not, Gideon wasn't immune to my competitive streak. When he was seven years old, I'd play Monopoly with him and cheat to make sure I could win. When he was ten and beating me at basketball, I'd pin him against the wall so that I could turn the score around.)

Gideon and I were living in an apartment on a street that bordered the Mormon Temple, a huge West Los Angeles landmark. If I wasn't drinking beer in my Jeep, which was often parked on the slope of our neatly manicured front lawn instead of in the parking area at the back, I might be walking up and down the street cutting pretty bouquets of flowers out of everybody else's gardens. Many evenings, drinks and cigarettes in hand, my drinking-pal neighbor and I would walk across the street to the Temple grounds, where I would press the buttons on all the statues to hear them talk. Once or twice I ran through the Temple parking lot—from car roof to car roof.

As if a measure of my state of mind, the more I drank, the more out of control my huge shoe collection would get, ending up in great heaping piles both inside and outside my closet. At one point, my roommate, Judith, took the entire situation in hand, helping me hang two shelves the full length of one wall in my bedroom. We then sorted the shoes—the boots with the boots, the workout shoes and high heels all lined up by style and color. My orderly shoes gave me hope, as if I could do the same with my thoughts, with the growing sense of craziness I felt in my life but didn't understand. It made me feel that my life was under control. It was an illusion.

Some people drink to feel loose; I drank not to feel at all. If alcohol made me act a little crazy, nuttiness had become a part of my personality, and it wasn't always easy to blame my actions on the bottle. Wine was my anesthetic of choice, and a half-gallon a day was typical. But I'd drink beer, too, and Bloody Marys or champagne on Sundays. I'd drink myself to sleep every night, but if the booze didn't act fast enough there was always Valium.

Nonetheless, I seldom slept through until morning. In the pattern set early in my childhood, I'd wake up in the middle of the night. I'd drink and smoke and eat, and occasionally Gideon or Judith would find me in the kitchen conducting a meeting with invisible companions. (Though I talked in my sleep and sleepwalked throughout most of my life, this has only recently been diagnosed as an eating/sleeping disorder. As a child, I had gone to the den at three in the morning to meet Arnold; now, my old hunger for love leads me to search for food. Judith recalls that she'd often be awakened in the dead of night by a popping sound. Going to investigate, she'd find me, sound asleep, shoving popcorn into my mouth as fast as it flew out of the air popper. A cruel twist of fate for someone fighting a lifelong battle against fat.)

In the morning, I'd get up and, fortified with coffee, go off to be an advertising executive and begin the cycle again. There's no telling how long that might have continued if my sister Victoria hadn't gotten married.

DRUNK

Nan and Arnold divorced when Vic was five, and I left the house when she was nine, first to go to the Academy and then to marry Tony. With Tony continually threatening to kill Victoria if I left him, I had stayed away from the family to protect her. But in the years since I left Tony, when Victoria and I both lived in California, we had grown increasingly close and shared warm feelings, wonderful experiences and lots of laughter. Until my drinking interfered.

Although we continued to see each other, Vic was scared and upset by my drinking. She felt that she couldn't trust me and worried about Gideon, probably with good reason, though I still didn't recognize that I had a problem.

On May 12, 1985, Victoria got married. True to her childhood dream, she had become an accomplished artist, and now she had found a man she loved who loved her dearly in return. They had a beautiful new home and the ceremony was held in their garden, Victoria wearing an amazing and unusual wedding dress crafted from soft leather. I was so excited for her and so proud.

Gideon and I went to the wedding together. Of course Mother was there and Wendy and lots of friends. Victoria had made just one request of me: not to drink before or during her wedding. But I was beyond requests. I had a few glasses of champagne before leaving my house to muffle my emotions, I drank a lot at the wedding, and I left a couple of times with a man whose name I don't remember and went down to the Saddle Peak Lodge for more champagne. I got drunk.

I remember standing in the living room with one hand on my hip and the other holding a drink, saying to Gideon, "I bet you never saw your mother like *this* before." (My daytime drinking was normally a private affair.) My beautiful little sister Victoria stood there alongside her new husband, surrounded by family and friends, and frowned at me for my drunken behavior. I responded by throwing my purse and shoes at her. Leaving Gideon behind, I climbed into the man's convertible with him, and we drove away.

Later on, Wendy dropped Gideon off at home, and I was still with this man. Hearing Gid come in, we got up, and the three of us went out for ice cream, as if everything were just peachy.

When I woke up the next morning, I knew that I had crossed some kind of line. Victoria called me, furious. I can't remember what she said except that she told me that she had called my therapist and told her what had happened. Dr. A., who had been my staunchest ally in assuring me that I didn't have a drinking problem, now reversed her position and told me that I was indeed an alcoholic.

Once I was officially an alcoholic, I gathered up all my bottles and hid them—on high shelves in the closet, in the toilet tank, in the oven. I refused to leave my room. I didn't even call in to work. I was done. I was cooked. I had had enough. I didn't comb my hair or brush my teeth. I called Steve and Simon and told them that they had to take care of Gideon because I was unfit and Stupid and just wanted to die.

Dr. A. said that I needed to go into a rehab program. In my drunken fog, I somehow comprehended that I had to get away from Gideon, to protect him. If I ever wanted to be part of a family again, I would have to leave home and get cleaned up. So, with the help of my next-door drinking buddy and his girlfriend, I found myself headed for detox. My friend Dawn would stay with Gideon at the apartment. My neighbor drove me to the hospital, and I made her go with me into the coffee shop so I could have one more beer. I was loaded when I checked in. It was May 15, 1985. A week later, Gideon turned thirteen without me.

Those first days are still a blur. I was not just detoxing from alcohol, but from sleeping pills as well. I hadn't gone to sleep without help for over twenty years; it was a skill I would have to learn all over again.

As soon as I got to my room, I hid in the closet. I didn't want to see or talk to anyone. I had *never* liked leaving home, never traveled and always arranged my life around my home. Now I was thrust into a completely unfamiliar place, without my son, without my wine, with people I had never seen before, and I was panicked. Everything, and everyone, frightened me. Just leaving my floor of the hospital to go to another floor for an Alcoholics Anonymous (A.A.) meeting traumatized me. If we planned a trip to the park, I would hide in the closet until the other patients would knock and tell me it was okay, I could come out.

I could no longer maintain the soft focus of my drunkenness. Everything became sharp and clear. I was Fat and Stupid and Ugly, and I couldn't hide it anymore.

Gradually I emerged, followed the rules, went to my meetings and saw the therapist. And over the course of days or weeks, Century City Hospital became a safe place. After all those years of drinking, having a name for what I was—alcoholic—struck me as amazing and miraculous. But it was so hard. In one family therapy session with Mother, we were told to write something we had never shared with each other. She wrote, "What did your father do to you? Tell me, I know." I wrote, "I want to tell you what happened with my father." We left group therapy and went back to my room. She got into bed with me, and we cried and told each other things that we remembered, and things that had never been said aloud between us.

I was permitted a few visitors. Dawn came and brought Gideon and stuffed animals. My boss from one of the real estate companies came, and I took him on a tour, and we played Ping-Pong. He told another friend how happy I was in the hospital.

After forty days, I was released to begin the real work of being a sober alcoholic. It was much harder being out than it was being in the hospital. I went to A.A. meetings every day. For the first year, just walking through those A.A. doors was painful. I didn't want to be in some room meeting with a bunch of strangers; I wanted to be at home. As friendly as people were, they still scared me. I would sit alone and often found myself in tears. Then I found Papa Joe and sat with him in the back row, safe. He helped me find my way.

Sometime in the first year, Charlotte became my sponsor. She was always a vision in pink, and I did everything she told me, but I couldn't speak up. Any time someone asked me to read the simplest thing, I would cry and run out the door. The closest I came to drinking again was when I had been sober a year, and Charlotte asked me to lead the Sunday meeting. I said no and spent the entire day in the closet crying. I was way too ugly and way too stupid to stand up in front of a roomful of people.

Charlotte sponsored about eight women and brought me in to her little "gang" of recovering alcoholics. We'd share our stories and our feelings and gradually grew to be good friends. We'd sit together at meetings and encourage each other. I began to feel less alone and to see how my drinking had made it easier for me to feel invisible. The *real* Debrah was Fat, Stupid, Ugly, and deeply damaged. But the *drinking* Debrah had a great job, real skills, good friends, a loving family—and a terror of being revealed as an imposter. I realized that I had found another closet—it came in the shape of a bottle.

My next sponsor was Clancy. He was an old-timer, a major circuit speaker for A.A. and a huge influence on me. He directed me to call him every day at 1:30 P.M., no matter where I was. In a meeting, on the freeway, it didn't matter, I'd have to stop what I was doing and call him; he would listen to me, grunt and hang up, and somehow I knew he understood.

If I wouldn't read or speak at a meeting, I was happy to accept any other sort of commitment. I served coffee, brought food, set up chairs—almost anything else. And by going to the same meetings and seeing the same people again and again, I eventually overcame my fear and learned to read and to share my story. The first few times, I trembled like a baby bird. I never came to enjoy it, but I was able and willing to participate, and I learned that telling my story not only helped me, but it also helped other people. Just as hundreds of other speakers had inspired me, every time I spoke, somebody would tell me how my words had helped them to do something that they couldn't do before.

Although I was learning to share my feelings, I felt terribly exposed. Sobriety didn't make my history disappear, but it did help me to see that I wasn't the only one haunted by the past. People in A.A. were wonderful and caring and understanding. I worked the steps. I took my inventories and made my amends. After three years, I started sponsoring other women. We'd work the steps together, they would call me every day, and we'd meet as a group every week. As my life changed, I got to watch their lives change, one day at a time.

All I know is that sobriety and A.A. gave me another chance at life—a chance to be a good mother, a good sister and a good friend. It gave me a chance to find truly meaningful work, and when things were difficult, it gave me the knowledge that if I could get sober, I could survive anything. I couldn't undo the damage that had been done, but sobriety gave me a chance to make repairs, to be grateful and to experience hope.

REAL LIFE

Without my protective doses of numbness, I emerged from detox raw and vulnerable. And totally broke. My credit cards had been charged to the hilt before I went into rehab, and then the insurance company rejected the hospital's $35,000 bill. After trying everything else, I declared bankruptcy. As usual—as I was now increasingly able to see—Gideon was the one who paid the highest price, having to leave the excellent private school where he was enrolled with friends he had known for years and transfer to a public school.

As soon as I got out of the hospital, I went back to work in real estate, now at a different company, and my days became regular rounds of office, A.A. meetings and home to bed.

Through A.A., I met Harry and had my first, brief, sober relationship. He had beautiful blue eyes, was a fabulous A.A. speaker and clearly taken with me. But one morning

I woke up in his bed on his boat, looked at his aged white skin next to mine, and the hair on my arms stood up. I suddenly realized that he was as old as my father would have been. I rushed out and later wrote him a letter explaining that I couldn't see him anymore.

Until then, I had successfully denied my memories of Arnold's abuse. The experience with Harry released a flood of horror into my life. Walking my dog near my apartment, I glanced up at a second-story window and saw my father (who had died more than fifteen years before) standing there, telling me to slice my throat open—to shut me up so I couldn't tell anyone what he had done to me. Back home, I was shaken to the core and holding a knife in my hand when the phone rang. I picked it up. It was my friend and former boss, Jon Douglas. I told him what had happened, and he said, "You go right now and see your therapist from the hospital; I'll pay for it." And he continued to pay for my therapy, three times a week for five years.

Dr. Baker was not only experienced with drug and alcohol abusers, but he was also a sensitive and insightful therapist. He was able to make the connection between my reaction to Harry, my hallucinatory "message" from Arnold and the abuse, thus opening a long and productive therapeutic relationship. My years of therapy with Dr. Raymond and Dr. A. had focused on just getting me through, from one day to the next. At long last, with excruciating pain, I began to look at the most frightening parts of my past.

Talking about the abuse was, at every moment, both

good and bad. Just as I had been amazed to discover that my disease had a name—alcoholism—I now found the words to describe my father's predatory behavior. At the same time, as every word slipped out of my mouth, I was certain that I would be struck down—that Arnold would sweep in from the past to prevent me from telling the truth. He never came. I kept talking. And it never really got any easier.

Very slowly, I began to recover emotionally and financially.

One evening at an A.A. meeting, after I had taken a cake for my third A.A. birthday, a burly African-American man came up to me wearing the little blue hat and blue two-piece outfit that people get when they're released from prison. He said, "I know your son, Gideon," and I thought, *Oh god, Gideon's dealing drugs.* How could he possibly know Gideon? And he said, "I'm Jimmy. I work with Gideon in the mailroom at Jon Douglas Company."

He walked out to the car with me, and we talked, and I said that he could come to see me take another A.A. birthday cake the next day. After we had gone to a few meetings together, one evening he asked if he could court me. That was the word he used. Except for my abortive relationship with Harry, I hadn't gone out with anyone since I had gotten sober, and I thought it would be okay to start dating a little.

We talked for hours. Jimmy came to my apartment, dressed in a suit, hat and everything, carrying flowers, looking very snazzy. We watched a movie. We made out. Significantly, when I looked at his tattooed brown skin, I didn't see my father.

After a while, Jimmy moved in. Gideon was not happy. There hadn't been a man in our house since I left Simon, and Gid was now a junior in high school, and this was a person he worked with. It was very difficult for him. He wasn't driving yet but started spending less time at home and more time out of the house with his friends. Having already survived a roller-coaster lifetime of ups and downs, he was finally beginning to show some resentment.

Although I was sober, I was still not much of a mom for Gideon. If I was now able to drive him around with both eyes open, I was overwhelmed with the demands of sobriety, therapy and keeping my fragile self from flying into a million pieces. Gideon had somehow survived on my love, which was as intense as ever, and the kindness of his stepfather. He had a wonderful and eclectic group of friends, who had often been visitors in our apartment, but it was only later that I found out that he wasn't spending all of his school days in school.

Jimmy was essentially raised in prison and had spent most of his life there for various petty crimes. That's probably why we connected so well: his prison cell and my closet. We were together but separate. We respected each other's boundaries and limitations. We lived in Mar Vista in a beautiful, top floor apartment with all the amenities, including a gorgeous marble-tiled shower. But every day Jimmy continued to put on his rubber flip-flops, take his underwear into the shower, wash it, wring it out and hang it up to dry. He kept his toothpaste and toothbrush on a separate shelf outside the bathroom. Prison training. He never went to school. It's amazing that he managed to escape his past—his troubled family, his incarcerations—and move on to a productive life.

When I was three years sober, I quit smoking. Forever.

Except for my pregnancy, when I put my baby first and managed to stop smoking *and* drinking, I had smoked through good times and bad. I smoked when my beautiful son asked me not to. I smoked through cancer and marriages and divorces and right on into my sobriety, where I found myself surrounded by equally cigarette-fixated alcoholics. I simply saw myself as a smoker, even doing a self-portrait weaving in which I have a cigarette hanging out of my mouth.

I was a smoker for life at the rate of two and a half packs a day.

I had actually tried to quit. Any number of times. I tried hypnosis and tapes and classes and drugs and challenges from friends and family. Sometimes I was successful for a little while, but as soon as I took a drink, I'd want a cigarette, and that would be that.

I was living with Jimmy and trying yet once more to stop, this time getting rid of all my ashtrays and chewing Nicorette gum. I probably chewed the nicotine equivalent of five packs a day, but I had told Gideon (again) that I would quit. I was determined. But then I would be desperate for a smoke, so I'd offer to go out and buy Jimmy some ice cream. I'd drive to the store and sneak a cigarette, and of course, I'd get caught.

Jimmy would say, "Go on, have another cigarette. I'll

just buy you new ashtrays and put them all over the house, and then I'll take Gideon, and we'll sign your death certificate. You don't care, why should we?" Then he would prepare to yell for Gideon.

This happened at least a half-dozen times, and then one day, I just stopped smoking. That was 1988, and I haven't smoked since.

But there's seldom a day when I don't *want* to smoke. I dream of smoking and never mind sitting next to smokers. Smoking was *much* more important than drinking, and stopping was *much* more difficult. Even if I was Fat, Stupid and Ugly, I could make Arnold proud of me by being a good smoker. I will always want to smoke, each breath affirming my father's twisted love, cinching tighter the grip he continues to hold on my memories and my mind. Quitting was the hardest thing I've ever done.

Jimmy and I spent five years together. We'd get up every morning at 4:30 A.M. and work out at World Gym with all the other gym rats. We went to the beach, where he would run, and I would skate. We ate meals together, went to A.A. meetings and movies, and visited his family, whose life made South Central Los Angeles look like Beverly Hills. He had a sweet, lovely daughter who stayed with us at various times. When they were occasionally released from prison, his brothers would visit, until eventually they'd steal some money or do something else that upset Jimmy, and he'd send them away.

Jimmy decided he had to have a Great Dane. We went to look at dogs, and who could resist those floppy little puppies, all ears and paws. He was in love, so we got Bruno and Phantom, one tan, one black. We spent a lot of time walking those dogs, hanging onto their leashes as they practically dragged us down the street. As big as Jimmy was, they were bigger. It was like having two giant children.

One day I woke up in bed with Jimmy, all toasty under the covers, and before I opened my eyes I was talking to him about what we could do that morning—get up and go for a cappuccino and go down to the beach and so on—and then from the other side of the room I hear Jimmy's voice saying, "Who are you talking to?" And I leaped up, only to discover that I had been lying butt-to-butt with Phantom, thinking it was Jimmy.

In the early morning of January 17, 1994, I was jolted awake from a sound sleep when Jimmy hurled himself on top of me in bed and hung on for dear life. Everything was creaking and clattering around us as the Northridge earthquake shook and heaved our apartment back and forth. My big boyfriend and my big dogs were terrified. The shaking went on for a long time. We were lucky. We didn't have any major damage, but we also didn't have any power, and once the sun came up, we had quite a struggle getting Bruno and Phantom down the dark, narrow stairwell to the street, three flights below.

UGLY

I was born ugly. My mother had carefully noted it in my baby book and I knew it from the time I was a tiny child. My father hurled the word at me again and again, and it was as much a part of my identity as "Debbie." Except for my grandmothers, no one ever said anything to the contrary.

Growing up, I carried a terrible burden of shame, knowing that I was too ugly for other people to look at. I would turn up my collar, try to hide my face, and went out of my way to avoid seeing my reflection in a mirror.

I was the Ugly Duckling, but I continually failed to turn into a swan. I looked at my mother and my sisters, who were all beautiful, and I was certain that I was adopted. How could those beautiful people be related to *me*? I searched the house for adoption papers, convinced that they would reveal the truth.

After I had been sober for a few years, I was having some breathing problems, so my doctor referred me to an ear, nose and throat specialist. He examined me and found that I had a deviated septum; we talked about my problems sleeping and the possibility of sleep apnea. Then he asked if anything else bothered me and I said, "My neck!"

He said, we can fix your neck easily. All you need is some liposuction and maybe I can add a little bit to your chin. I really didn't know the first thing about plastic surgery, but all I could say was yes, yes, yes!

I checked his references and checked myself into the hospital for an overnight stay. He fixed my deviated septum, gave me a little chin implant, snipped a tiny bit off the end of my nose and took two cups of fat out of my neck. (For comparison, a pound of butter is two cups of fat.) Healing was easy. I wore a chin wrap for a few days and felt like an overnight miracle.

Interestingly, as dramatic as the change felt to me, almost none of my friends or business associates noticed the difference. But that didn't matter. *I* noticed. No Neck had a neck. I had focused on my ugly neck for so long, and it had vanished.

The fat never returned to my neck, the chin stayed put and my nose didn't grow. On the other hand, I was still Ugly, and that may never change. When people compliment me, I believe that they are patronizing me, or lying. It would take a lot more than plastic surgery to erase the psychological scarring of the Ugly label I've worn since birth, but this simple procedure did make me feel more confident, more capable and, if not more attractive, at least somewhat less horrible. I was myself, but better.

WORK, PART THREE

From 1987 to 1993, I worked for Jon Douglas again. Back in familiar territory, I continued to create advertising and public relations campaigns that would enhance the company's image. But, increasingly, I found my focus turning away from the repetitive daily routines of an advertising department to the more personal and meaningful arena of community affairs.

Jon Douglas (better known as Jack) had over the years become a close friend. He believed in me both personally and professionally. (One Christmas, when I was strapped for funds, Jack piled my car full of presents, skis and a Christmas tree, and sent Gideon and me up to Big Bear to celebrate.) I loved my job and title: Director of Community Affairs. Organizations would come to me asking for money, and I would go to Jack and ask *him* for money; it was like being his wife and asking for a fur coat. I would say I found a wonderful project, and I need

$5,000 for this foundation or that library or to help children. And when I told him he needed to make a donation to this charity or take a position on the board of that one, he accepted my advice. He put money into each of the communities where he had offices.

My lifelong urge to protect small, defenseless beings inspired my special concern for the welfare of children, older people, and the homeless, so most of our efforts went in that direction. In 1988, along with millions of other people I was deeply moved by the movie *Stand and Deliver*, which told the story of Jaime Escalante, a calculus teacher whose determination had yielded academic miracles among his students at Garfield High School in East Los Angeles. Not long after the movie was released, an article in the *Los Angeles Times* profiled a teacher who was taking a similar approach at South Central's Jefferson High School.

Jack had been funding sports teams and scholarships in the affluent communities where he had offices, but when I asked him if he would fund a teacher in the inner city, he said yes. I figured that instead of helping one child, we could support a teacher who would help dozens. So I wrote a note and sent it with a basket of cookies and milk to this Jefferson High School teacher and his students, thinking that we could buy something for their classroom, such as books or a copier. After a long delay, the teacher finally called me back and said he didn't *want* our money. He wanted me to come to South Central to meet him and the children. I wasn't eager to leave my office, but this was such an oddball sort of response that I arranged a meeting.

He said the children need *you*, a connection with a real person outside South Central. He kept insisting, "I don't want your *money*, I want your *time*." I didn't exactly understand what he meant, but I could tell that he was sincere and that he believed in the children.

So I started working with his students from Jefferson High. I involved them in all of our community affairs activities. They walked with our sales agents and staff in AIDS Walk Los Angeles. We took a busload of children to Malibu where we all ran a 10K race; their teacher, who didn't own sneakers, gamely ran along in his street shoes.

The children helped us staff events that we sponsored and collect toys, blankets and clothing for homeless families. We took them to downtown L.A.'s skid row where they interviewed and videotaped homeless people and then wrote papers on what it was like to be homeless. They served dinner for seniors at holiday events. I was a board member for various charities, and the children attended meetings with me.

They got awards for what they were doing. They got their pictures in the paper and were recognized by their peers and the community. One of the children, Elena, became my informal little sister. Elena, Gideon and I went everywhere together. She invited me to visit her home and meet her family. That was really my first personal experience with the profound poverty of South Central. She showed me her world; I showed her mine.

We mentored each other. When I was promoted to Vice President of Marketing, Elena became Student Body Vice President at Jefferson High School, later going on to college and a teaching career.

I took Gideon along on my trips to South Central, and he got to learn what it was like in the "hood." We brought kids from the inner city to work at Jon Douglas Company as paid interns, and Jack appeared as a speaker at several events at Jefferson.

I promoted all of these activities in the Jon Douglas offices and looked for agents who would "adopt" one of the children. We set up an informal mentoring program. The agents would pick up the children in South Central and bring them to their offices, explain their work, take them out to restaurants and movies, and help them with their homework. I don't know whose lives changed more, the children's or the agents'. Most of these youngsters had never been outside of the impoverished and gang-infested neighborhoods of South Los Angeles. They had never been in a high-rise building or seen the Pacific Ocean, just ten miles from where they lived. On the other hand, the agents quickly discovered that these students were not faceless statistics or monsters to be feared; they were *children*.

In 1989, we recruited gyms around town to cooperate with us in a "Workout for the Homeless" day, where hundreds of people made a small contribution and worked out for an hour at their favorite gym. Building on that event, in 1990, we successfully petitioned Los Angeles

Mayor Tom Bradley to name November 17 as "Workout for the World Day." With seventy gyms involved statewide, we expanded the number of beneficiaries and attracted numerous television and sports personalities as well as media attention. We took the children in vans to the various sites to hand out T-shirts and explain where the money was going.

During this time, I was always working out at one gym or another, and one day a friend said, you really should try yoga. While I thought it sounded way too slow and boring for me, in 1991 I finally agreed to give it a try. Bryan Kest was the teacher, and his program was called Power Yoga. It was not slow or boring. It was *brutal*. Red-faced and exhausted, I hurt all over. But I love a challenge, especially a physical one, and I kept going to classes. Before long, Bryan became interested in the work I was doing in South Central. He put together a yoga class for 300 kids in the gym at Jefferson High School and continued working with South Central youth, including gang members, winning a place in my heart forever.

I loved my community affairs work, and I loved the children. I felt that I was at home, just like I had felt at home with the juvenile delinquents I befriended growing up. These South Central children accepted me, laughed with me and opened their hearts to me. They didn't find me intolerably fat, stupid or ugly. They needed me as much as I needed them.

I was now earning $100,000 a year working for Jon Douglas, but I realized that I wanted to work at a job that focused exclusively on helping children. I wanted that more than I wanted my salary. So I subscribed to the *Chronicle of Philanthropy* and started sending out resumes. With my experience creating successful programs, raising money and getting huge amounts of media attention, I thought I'd be a plum for some children's charity. I sent out dozens of letters, which quickly piled up and turned into hundreds. Nobody was interested in hiring me. I was surprised and discouraged.

I thought maybe the Los Angeles public television station, KCET, might find a position for me in children's programming. So I arranged a meeting with David Crippens, whom I had met when KCET co-sponsored an event with Jefferson High School and Jon Douglas Company. David asked, "What do you really want to do with your life?" It was the first time anyone had ever asked me that question. I had never had a dream or a goal. I had worked to support myself, and then myself and Gideon, and had simply moved from one job to the next, one idea to the next, up and down, throughout my life.

But my answer was there, just waiting for the right question. I said, "All I want to do is open a safe house for the children from Jefferson. A safe place where they can get off the street after school, have a snack, do their homework and play."

He said, "You can do that." I thought, *No I can't; I didn't even graduate from high school.* He said, "Write this down: 501(c)(3). You go find a place, look up information on raising money and do it. That's all."

The next day, I told Jack that I was going to quit my job and make this idea happen. In yet another grand demonstration of friendship and generosity, he gave me six months' severance pay and the use of an office and a phone. I left the office, picked up Juliana, one of my A.A. sponsees, and over coffee, told her my idea and asked her if she would help. A man who had been sitting at the table behind us got up and dropped his business card on our table. He said, call me and I'll help you get your federal 501(c)(3) tax-exemption. I did, and he did, in a record thirty days. He also helped me come up with the name: A Place Called Home.

It was early 1993.

FINDING A PLACE CALLED HOME

The next six months went by in a fever of excitement and anxiety. I recruited a few of the young women I sponsored in A.A. to assist me, and we spent every waking hour trying to create something out of nothing.

I didn't have a clue what I was doing. We had to learn everything from scratch. We chased down information about grants and gave ourselves a crash course in grant writing. We sent letters to anyone—friends, relatives, businesses, foundations—who might possibly be sympathetic. We launched a P.R. campaign, mailing press releases to the papers every week. I asked the Jon Douglas Company sales staff for contributions and worked through the list of just about every real estate agent I'd ever known. Some agents donated money; others donated gorgeous clothes that we'd sell at lively garage sales. We put together packets and sent those out. Hundreds of them. We went to the California

Community Foundation and wrote down everything we could find that might help us.

It was haphazard at best. When I look back, I can see that we weren't doing it right, we were just doing it. I figured that if we got some money and found a location, the children would show up. I wasn't wrong; I was just naive. We didn't get very much money. We got a little help from some brave foundations and a few really visionary individuals. A check for $300 was like a miracle. Our budget was $30,000 a year, and most of it came out of my severance pay.

Right across the street from Jefferson High was a church. In working with the children and their families, I had become acquainted with the minister, Reverend Jupiter, so I went to see him and told him what I was doing. There was a house on the church property, and he said we could rent it until we found something better. It was old and rundown, but that didn't matter. We signed a lease, and my mother and ten other volunteers came and scrubbed the place.

I put together a brochure describing each room: study room, weaving room, yoga/exercise room, kitchen for snacks, and twelve-step room. We sent out this twenty-page photocopied booklet with our continuing requests for funds. We painted the walls, installed fire extinguishers and an alarm system, and in September 1993, we opened the doors of A Place Called Home (APCH). A dozen children showed up.

We started offering Saturday morning yoga workouts

with Bryan Kest, spreading the word through the children I knew from Jefferson. I felt right at home. He'd teach yoga, and I'd serve bagels and cream cheese.

We kept on providing food and yoga classes and a quiet spot off the street to any child who wanted to come in. The first twelve came back and brought their friends. I discovered that these tough-looking "gangbangers," boys and girls alike, melted in the presence of a teddy bear, so I put out a call for bears, and we distributed those to all of the kids. We asked for sweatshirts, roller skates, televisions and typewriters, and we got those, too. The checks trickled in.

Then the church kicked us out. As Reverend Jupiter witnessed the signing of our incorporation papers, a photographer captured the moment in a picture that was turned into evidence against us: the elders thought that he had sold the church to me. On Mother's Day, we discovered that flyers had been left on all the cars in the church parking lot, saying that we were cultists and to stay away from us. We had a big meeting in the church to attempt reconciliation, but it was clear: they wanted us out. The children cried.

Reverend Jupiter was so upset by his congregation's actions that he took us up the block to see about another church and to meet his friend Bishop Richardson. Bethel Church of Christ had a big subterranean parking area and a large space upstairs. They met with all their board members, who said that we could move in and made us feel welcome, so we packed up and started over. We had to forfeit the money we had spent on improvements.

We used the Bethel Church parking area as a gym, and in three rooms upstairs found a place for the televisions and computers, meeting and office spaces, a quiet area for studying and a spot to serve food. We were in the church for four years and that was where A Place Called Home really took form.

To become a member of APCH, the children had to sign a written pledge, agreeing to ten rules that haven't changed since we opened our doors: no smoking, no drinking, no drugs, no weapons, no graffiti, no racism, no fighting, no profanity, no gang-related "colors" and no gang-related apparel.

Our earliest members were high-school age and we stretched the age range at the upper end to include older children who were out of school and had no place to go. If they weren't gang members themselves, almost every child had at least one gang member in their family, often more. Most lived well below the poverty line; many had parents and siblings in prison or otherwise missing from their lives. Many had seen their friends and family members gunned down in gang warfare and drive-by shootings. The pressures and dangers of the street were, and are, powerful and unrelenting.

APCH sits in the middle of an almost entirely Latino neighborhood, but from the very beginning, for reasons we were never able to fathom, we attracted both Latino and African-American children. On the street, these children were in rival gangs, and at first they brought their hostilities indoors. The Latino children would sit together in one area, the African-American children in another. But eventually they started bringing in their younger brothers and sisters and with more and more younger children around, the gangbangers became protective—they didn't seem to mind getting hurt themselves, but they didn't want the little ones to be injured. After a while, they started playing and working together and slowly discovered that, inside APCH, they could be, if not best friends, at least not mortal enemies.

If relations inside APCH thawed somewhat, open conflict still reigned in the street. In one memorable pre-Christmas confrontation at the church, gang members seemed to materialize from nowhere: children with guns. They hefted automatic weapons that some of them could barely lift. Someone came to get me. The staff and other children went running off to find a place to hide before the shooting began. I walked outside, right into the midst of the snarling and the guns, and said, "You put your guns down right now, or we're not going to celebrate Christmas, and you're not going to get any gifts." They did.

Again and again, I see how little it takes to distract the children from their habits of violence. A videotape, a music lesson, a basketball game, a snack or the promise of a Christmas gift, and the warrior transforms, right before your eyes, into an eager child.

Whatever they were, dropouts or straight-A students, angry-looking hoodlums, underfed street urchins or six-foot-four teenagers, they all had one thing in common:

when it came right down to it, they were children. And like children everywhere, they responded to attention, games, laughter and all the food we could serve them.

The step-by-step tools that I had learned in A.A. became a model for some of the work we did at APCH. I took the children who had drug, alcohol and gang problems to A.A. meetings with me. I'd fill the van with kids, and we'd go to a meeting and then out to lunch. I loved it and so did they. We set up A.A. meetings at the center, and I would bring in speakers for them. We started Gangsters Anonymous, where, for the first time, hard-core gang members could speak honestly about the challenges they faced. Even Dr. Baker, who had helped me get sober, volunteered as a therapist and a consultant at APCH until he moved away from the area.

Among the early members of APCH were Monique and Lawrence. Sister and brother, they were very close, living at home with their crack-addict mother and showing up at APCH every day after school. Beautiful, tall, slender Monique, always wearing her headphones, was captain of the Jefferson High School basketball team and a great student. She would come in and do her homework, never smiling and never speaking to anyone. But when she spoke, she had a foul mouth, and with a flip of her wrist, she could incite gang warfare. As tough and mean as Monique could be, Lawrence was all smiles, a sweet, loving child without a mean bone in his body.

Each evening, as we locked the doors at A Place Called Home, Monique and Lawrence would wait for me, and I'd drive them to the bus stop, where they'd board a bus and ride halfway across town to their home. People were always donating clothing to APCH, and I would find beautiful coats and sweaters for Monique. She'd try them on, but I'd never see her wearing them again. Everything I gave her disappeared from her closet, sold for drug money by her mother.

One evening, someone called APCH looking for Monique's mother because Monique was in jail for assaulting a player from another team; she had thrown a bottle at someone who had called her a nigger. Lawrence and I went to the jail to get Monique released, and I signed as her guardian. After that, she opened up a bit and seemed more trusting.

I felt absolutely at ease with the children at A Place Called Home. Their lives were surrounded by a horrifying but nonetheless adrenaline-pumping kind of risk and danger that I could relate to. Everything that had happened in my life prepared me for this work. I identified with them, felt compassion for them and loved them without reservation.

If my friends expressed puzzlement or concern at my willingness to drive my car into South Central and spend every day working there, I never felt any fear. In fact, I often say that getting off the freeway at Central Avenue is like being in Hawaii—I feel like I'm on vacation. It's not beautiful, but for me, it's relaxing, it's safe and it's where my heart is most filled with love.

We started to get some awards and recognition. In

March 1994, I was invited to the White House to attend President Clinton's presentation of the Anti-Violent Crime Initiative. I took along three teenagers who had never been out of Los Angeles, flown in a plane or stayed in a hotel. We spent two memorable days sightseeing in the nation's capital.

Slowly, our membership grew, our programs expanded and our donations ticked upward. People saw articles in the paper and became volunteers. I was surrounded by friends. Juliana, who had helped me from the moment the idea of APCH began, was now on the staff (and still is). Jimmy was the security guard.

Mother interviewed hundreds of children, transcribing their stories and writing poetry about them. She continued volunteering once a week for eight years. Every summer, vanloads of kids swam in her pool and ate her barbecued lunches, calling her Grandma. (Through the children's eyes, and my own slow healing, I came to see Nan as a caring, energetic woman. She is devoted to the children and generous with her time and energy. She wants to be my mother; but just as I can't correct my mothering of Gideon, Nan can't undo her failure to mother me. We can work together, but we are still struggling to be mother and daughter.)

I had found more than A Place Called Home; I had found *my* home. In starting APCH, my life filled with living dolls of every shape, size and color. And just like all the dolls that went before them, they accepted and returned the love and protection I lavished upon them.

A year after we opened our doors, I decided that I wanted to live closer to APCH, so I packed up the Great Danes and moved into a huge pink house in South Central Los Angeles.

SOUTH CENTRAL

Without much help from me, Gideon had graduated from high school and gone off to college in Santa Barbara. He was seriously in love for the first time. I had been sober for six years and had found my life's work. Things were going exceptionally well.

The word "Home" in the name of our youth center kept pulling at me. I envisioned living in a comfortable place that the children could visit when our center at the church was closed. I also wanted to live among the people I worked with. I didn't want to be the white lady who came in from the Westside, an outsider. I wanted to be a neighbor, to shop at the same stores, to meet the children and their parents on the streets in the community where they lived. When I found the pink house behind Hoover Park, it fit right into the picture.

It was huge, a restored Adams District Victorian house with five bedrooms, including a master suite with a sitting room and enormous balcony. There was no heat except for the fireplaces, but it had acres of antique wallpaper, amazing wood moldings and high ceilings. Outside, there was a large backyard with a sleeping studio and a guest house that I turned into a game room, plus a front yard and fencing all the way around. Thousands of avocado trees populate South Central's backyards, and the pink house had a gigantic, prolific tree that would drop hundreds of avocados, which Bruno and Phantom would eat practically before the fruit hit the ground.

I leased the house and moved in with Jimmy and the Great Danes. I felt safe there and didn't notice the gunshots or circling helicopters, but Jimmy was rattled and confessed after living there a short time that he was too scared. A few weeks later, he moved out. And so we split up amicably and remain friends to this day.

Monique and Lawrence were very excited when I asked if they wanted to help us unpack and then spend the night at the pink house. I told them to check with their mother. A big crowd of friends and APCH members helped us with the move; it was hard work and great fun. At the end of the day, Monique claimed one of the bedrooms, which would later be called the princess room, and Lawrence settled into another.

The next morning, we drove up to APCH, opened the gate, and there was their mother, screaming at me for taking her children. She was in bad shape. I talked to her about sobriety and told her that if she went into rehab I would be happy to take care of the children until she straightened out, and she agreed. The children had been taken away from her many times; each time it was worse, for them and for her. She saw my offer as an easy solution. But then their social worker showed up and said that the children were already "part of the system," and if their mother went into rehab, they would pull the children out of Jefferson and separate them; Monique would live with her aunt and Lawrence would move in with someone else in Riverside (in the next county).

I was outraged. All these children had was each other and their friends and commitments at school. I turned where I had always turned when I had a problem that needed attention: the media. I made phone calls to news stations and politicians; the papers picked it up and Channel 9 did a huge, heartwarming story.

Thus I began the fight to become a foster parent. Monique and Lawrence continued to stay with me as I went through foster parent training and the endless documentation. I had no desire to run a home for foster children; I merely wanted to keep Monique and Lawrence together until their mother got sober.

But she couldn't seem to get herself straightened out, so I fostered the two children until Monique graduated from high school, two years of "Leave It to Beaver" domestic happiness. I cooked and cleaned and spent my weekends with Monique and Lawrence, who called me "Momma D." We shopped for clothes and books. We went to the movies. We watched TV together. They got enough to eat every day and knew that the things they brought home wouldn't disappear from their rooms. Sober, I was able to be the mother to Monique and Lawrence that I hadn't been to Gideon. Everyone at A Place Called Home called Monique my princess—a nickname that still sticks. She went from being tough, mean and foul-mouthed to softening her edges as she began to feel valued and loved. As she says, instead of having to be the responsible one in the family, she was able to be cared for and "feel like a kid" for the first time in her life.

When Gideon returned from Santa Barbara, he joined us in the pink house with his girlfriend and their two dogs. The two young women immediately disliked each other, and the two dogs didn't do much better with Bruno and Phantom. I saw Monique as the daughter I had always wanted, and Gideon's girlfriend was ready to claim the daughter role as her own. Gideon (who was enrolled in chiropractic college and would eventually graduate, becoming a gentle, talented healer) was working part-time at APCH; his girlfriend became a full-time staff member. The boundaries between home, family and work got more and more blurred.

Meanwhile, to complicate the situation further, I had become involved with Lewis, who also moved into the house. Then things seemed to escalate fairly quickly. Monique, who had a serious boyfriend of her own, got pregnant. The landlord put the pink house up for sale. Gideon, his girlfriend and their dogs rented an apartment across town. Monique graduated from high school, and she and Lawrence moved in with their older sister. And I went, with Lewis, from one of the happiest periods of my life directly into one of the most terrifying.

BAD LOVE

had met Lewis at an A.A. meeting. One day I took a couple of the children from APCH to a big meeting in West Los Angeles. As I was looking around, I noticed a gorgeous African-American man. He was very well-dressed and very good-looking. He started talking to the children, which got my attention instantly. *What a nice guy,* I thought, and asked him to join us for coffee after the meeting. I took the three of them for frozen yogurt, and we got acquainted.

He explained that he was staying at the nearby Veterans Administration hospital. I had no idea what that meant. I figured that he had some kind of medical problems. He was newly sober, in rehab and going to a lot of meetings, so we went to A.A. meetings together. He was very friendly and charming and always knew a lot of people at the meetings, where everyone seemed to like him. Before long, Lewis had moved out of the V.A.

and into the pink house in South Central.

Except for his A.A. friends, though, I began to notice that no one else could stand him. He hadn't done anything wrong yet, but Gideon didn't like him, nobody at APCH liked him, including Jimmy, and Monique thought he was bad, bad, bad. They said, stay away from him. But I just figured their attitudes were normal; I thought that they were probably jealous because I was paying too much attention to someone else.

When everyone moved out of the pink house, Lewis and I moved into an apartment at the beach in Venice. I went back to Rollerblading on the boardwalk and driving back and forth to South Central. Lewis worked on and off at assorted jobs. Gideon, who lived not far away, was now engaged. On July 22, 1995, Gideon got married, and Lewis was my date for the wedding, looking as handsome as ever. I was sober and excited about my new relationship and my work.

Things went along nicely for about a month. Then Lewis got drunk. He grabbed my hair and threw me across the room. He tore off my clothes and forced himself on me. He shouted and shoved. It was horrible. Then he'd sober up, apologize and be charming and loving. He'd select my clothes, gently help me get dressed and we'd be right back together. We had a violent fight in the car on Pacific Coast Highway. He was drunk, and I came very close to jumping out of the moving car. When we got home, he again pulled me by my hair as he dragged me across the room. (A skilled batterer, Lewis never left marks where they would be visible when I was dressed.) Another time as he was beating me, I picked up a small television and threw it at him. That made him even angrier. But always he'd follow this horrific abuse with affection—a pattern etched into my unconscious, a lure I couldn't resist.

One night, after a particularly brutal assault, I ended up at Gideon's apartment, and Lewis followed me. He was driving the APCH van, and I was driving my Jeep Wrangler, which I had parked in Gideon's garage and locked with a Club. Lewis pounded on the sliding glass door, ramming it with his shoulder and shattering the glass. Gideon and his new wife pepper-sprayed him. We called the police, but they never showed up. Then Lewis went down to the garage and managed to take the Jeep, Club and all. It turned out that, in his wild rage, he had had an accident in the van and had hit somebody. That was a whole police issue in itself.

Gideon just wanted Lewis locked up. He was afraid for me, but he was also afraid for himself and his bride. So when Lewis sobered up a few days later, the two of us took him back to the V.A. hospital, where he was admitted to the psych unit, and where, I then learned, he had been a resident when we met. Lewis was pleading with us: he didn't mean it; he loved me. Even as he was being admitted to the hospital, I still wanted a relationship with this man.

But as soon as we were apart, I started to see how sick our relationship was, and while he was locked up, I moved to another apartment a few blocks down. I didn't want Lewis there, but he found me, said he was sober and I let him move back in, always giving him another chance. Then it would start all over again: the beatings, the rapes, the screaming, the apologies, the tears, the reconciliation.

As with my experiences with Arnold and Tony, I kept my abusive relationship a secret from my family. If we had not had the confrontation at Gideon's apartment, it's possible that they never would have found out. But once Gideon knew, I had to tell my sisters. Victoria was angry and terrified, and Wendy was ready to jump on a plane and kill Lewis with her bare hands. I was sober, but I was out of my mind. I just kept going back to him. Nobody could talk to me about leaving him, not my son, not my sisters, not my friends. I thought everybody was crazy except me.

I took Lewis with me to see my therapist and even my psychic; they were both charmed by him, making me feel that I was the crazy one. One day, in fear, I ran out of the apartment, and Lewis, drunk, jumped on his motorcycle and chased me down the beachfront alleyway. I screamed for the police, who stopped him, then accompanied us back to the apartment and waited with me until he left, still drunk, on the motorcycle. Why they didn't arrest him, I could only guess: even they were charmed.

Finally, I kicked him out and moved to another apartment. The new place had a big metal security door; I wasn't going to let him hurt me again. I was sponsoring a young woman in A.A. who had access to her father's gun, which I borrowed. I had made up my mind: if Lewis walked through that door I would shoot him. He stayed away.

So I had managed to get rid of him. That was the end of Lewis, until one day I was Rollerblading in Venice and saw him sleeping on a bench like a bum. I got totally freaked out; I thought that he had left the city, but there he was.

I knew that I had been through something really awful, really disturbing. But after a while, things seemed to calm down, my bruises healed and I threw myself into my work at A Place Called Home.

Months passed. Then one day I got a call from a detective saying that Lewis had been arrested for rape and murder. He had killed a woman in another state and a forensic psychiatrist wanted to meet with all the ex-wives and girlfriends.

I had recently met Diana, and she was just becoming a trusted friend when I got this call and the frightening memory of what I had experienced came rushing back. She helped me through this very painful, emotional time and offered to go with me to what seemed like an inquisition. I never could have done it alone.

Lewis had had a lot of stories. He'd talk about various wives and children, but I never knew exactly what to believe. At the meeting, Diana and I were introduced to the five attractive, successful, professional women who had the courage to come forward. (There were others, possibly thirty or more, but they were too afraid to participate.) We each talked about what Lewis had done to us, the same pattern, over and over: saying the same words, ironing our clothes, dressing us, tying our shoes, staying home during the day while we went to work and battering us horribly. When it was happening to me, I hadn't thought of what he was doing as rape. But when I heard the other women echoing my own violent sexual experiences with him, I couldn't deny it any longer. I saw the truth. We talked about his brutality and his seductive charm. Shortly after he was with me, he had murdered his next girlfriend.

Some months after that meeting, Diana and I had to fly back for the trial. At the courthouse, ten minutes before the trial started, the gathering ex-wives and girlfriends were informed that Lewis had fired his attorney and would be acting as his own counsel. For a moment, the earth seemed to drop away from under our feet. I was terrified to come face to face with this maniac, to have to answer his questions. We all were. Pale and shaken, holding hands, we said a prayer and walked together to the courtroom, where we were admitted one at a time for our testimony.

Dressed in his orange prison jumpsuit, chained to his chair, Lewis questioned me. I don't think I could have been any better on the stand than I was. I explained exactly what happened. In the course of his questioning, he said, "Ms. Constance, what is your definition of rape?" And I said, "Well, when you grab somebody by the hair and throw them across the room onto the bed, rip off their clothes, and stick it in them, I call that rape." And I turned to the judge and told him that I would have blown Lewis' head off if he had come through my door one more time. The daughters of the dead woman cheered. Lewis was convicted of rape. Within six months, he was also convicted of murder.

In A.A., when a sober alcoholic takes a drink, it's called a "slip." In my recovery from the abuse by Arnold and Tony, Lewis was a serious and potentially fatal slip. It took time and help for me to acknowledge the connection between Lewis, Tony and Arnold. Lewis's physical abuse was an expression of love in the sick language that I understood. Each of them had gained my trust, and then betrayed it. Like Tony, he'd be loving, and in a flash, without provocation, he'd turn into a monster. He was charming, a great storyteller, a very good dresser, abusive and violent. Just like my father. Reflecting on it is still sickening. I thought I had come so far, learned so much, that somehow those were things that could never happen to me again.

But Lewis is the only person I was ever really frightened of. Sometimes I get out of the shower and I jump. I keep thinking that he's right behind me, that he's going to show up and that's going to be the end. I'm still afraid of him. I hope he stays locked up forever.

A PLACE CALLED HOME

I f "it takes a village" to raise a child, we quickly learned that it would take a flock of angels to operate a successful youth center. During our grand-opening celebration in 1993, one of our volunteers answered the phone and, turning to me, said, "It's for you—it's Johnny Carson." *Oh sure,* I thought, as I picked up the receiver, and a woman said, "I have Johnny Carson on the line for you, one moment please." It really *was* Johnny Carson, calling to say that he had seen an article in the paper, loved what I was doing, and he wanted to send me a small check showing his appreciation. A couple of days later, a check arrived in the mail. Mr. Carson became—and has remained—one of our angels.

I faxed letters to hundreds of foundations, describing what I was trying to do. The one that went to the Jacobs Family Foundation had the word *HELP!* handwritten in huge letters across the top. And help they did, in capital letters. They gave us funding as well as many hours of assistance from skilled development professionals who guided us through the world of strategic business planning and fundraising. They also introduced me to Arianna Huffington, and I wanted her on the board right away. I loved her energy. She threw her arms open and embraced A Place Called Home; I could see that she was a true-blue fighter for human rights.

Our mission is to provide at-risk youth with a secure, positive family environment where they can regain hope and belief, earn trust and self-respect, and learn skills to lead a productive life free of the gangs, drugs, and poverty that surround them.

For those first years, three large rooms in a South Los Angeles church seemed to be a dream come true. But it also showed us that the need would always far exceed our capacity to meet it. After four years, when we were able to relocate to a 10,000-square-foot building, we felt that we had unlimited space to expand our programs. But just a few short years later, there was hardly room to turn around, let alone grow.

Our programs focus on the needs of the children. Each day hundreds of children come through our doors looking for their friends, something to eat, help with their homework or just a quiet place to sit. We brought in volunteer tutors to assist with homework. From endless donations of used computers, we established a computer repair workshop; the child who repaired a computer could take it home. We set up sports teams, eventually taking them out to local parks to compete in youth leagues. We offered art and sewing classes, with take-home results. The children who want to play music or sing, can. The children who want ballet slippers or tap shoes and serious dance lessons, get them.

There was a young girl, one of our members, who didn't speak. We all tried to break through, to find a way to get Autumn to talk. One day Autumn and I were watching a tap class. I asked her if she would like to dance. She shrugged her shoulders. I asked if it would make any difference if I got her some dancing shoes, and again, she wouldn't answer. Then I said, "What if I gave you these tap shoes?" With a small smile on her face, she nodded her head. That changed her life. Six years later, at our Tenth Anniversary Gala, Autumn was not only one of our lead dancers, but also a tap soloist and captain of the dance team.

Our angels come in all shapes and sizes. We work hand-in-hand with mentors from HBO and Warner Bros. to introduce the children to a world of possibilities. When I first met Mayra, a gang member from a gang family, she was failing nearly every class. But beneath her black lipstick and shaved eyebrows redrawn in high arches over her dark eyes, I could still see the sweet young girl. Patiently, her mentor helped that girl emerge. Three years later, about to graduate from high school, Mayra is today enrolled in college-level courses at Trade Tech and mentoring a younger child as part of our in-house program. Her eyebrows have grown in and she wears just a touch of pink lipstick—a symbol of her newfound self-esteem. Through mentoring and our other programs, I get to watch these children grow. The change is a miracle—to me *and* to them.

Diana originally came to APCH when I invited her for a site visit. I wanted her to see for herself what I had been talking about. While she was there, a woman who had been assaulted on the street came running in, crying. A trained counselor, Diana was able to assist her—and quickly fell in love with the place; she and her husband joined my board of directors.

Then I converted a storage area into a private counseling room, gave Diana a desk, a lamp and a sofa, and brought the gangbangers in to meet with her, one by one. Counseling was a new concept for most of our community, and they were understandably skeptical. Trusting the wrong person could be a costly mistake. But I'd walk Juan or Leo into Diana's office and tell them to sit down. I'd say she's my friend, she's okay, you can talk to her, and then I'd walk out and close the door behind me.

At that time, my experience was that volunteers come and go. Diana was a volunteer therapist until one day I insisted that she resign from the board and become a paid employee. She did, and for two years was the sole counselor for everyone at APCH.

Today our members, their families and the APCH staff turn willingly to our counselors as they are learning about self-worth, making healthy choices and dealing with crises. With support from the Davidow Charitable

Foundation, Diana and her staff have now spent more than seven years sitting with the children, one by one, listening, asking the right questions and helping them find answers. With the door closed, away from the anxiety and the pressure of their peers, they learn to let down their guard and to talk about themselves. They learn what it's like to have someone listen. And they slowly discover that it isn't their guns or their gangs that make them special; everyone at APCH is unique, special and worth listening to.

Surrounded and inspired by these beautiful children, I began to make dolls. Assembled from socks, yarn and buttons, and dressed in clothes put together from scraps of fabric, these dolls are as unique and filled with personality as the people I see every day. They are every shade of color, male and female, children and adults, nuns, yoga teachers, brides, doctors and angels. As I'm creating, the fabric and yarn seem to take over, guiding my hands. I taught the children how to make dolls, as well as how to treat them with love and care. (When my poised, confident foster daughter, Monique, delivered an exquisite baby, Kenny—my grandson—I got to see that the lessons of loving had all been absorbed. My childhood doll, Tiny Tears, had allowed me to experience unconditional love for the first time—a lesson that has now come full circle as it is passed along to children who discover that they, too, can practice loving and being loved in return.)

I'm so proud of my princess, Monique. She joined the staff in 1997 and helped us develop a program to bring

Christmas to the inner city. Today she works full time as the APCH Youth Leadership Director and is amazingly organized as she juggles family, college and work. Monique's son, Kenny, has been raised with his APCH family. By age five, he was shooting pool with the big kids, and now, at eight, he loves reading and basketball and his mom makes sure his homework is done every night. Nearly every time I walk through the doors of A Place Called Home, I hear "Grandma, Grandma!" and there's my Kenny.

There was no formula for the evolution of APCH. While we aggressively seek attention in the media, many of our angels are drawn by word of mouth. Our doors are open, and we never know who might show up. It could be the Lakers or the Clippers or other sports figures, television or movie stars, rap artists, politicians, clergy, college students or creative community members with time and ideas to share.

When Tupac Shakur was arrested, we learned that Tupac wanted to do something for APCH as part of his community service. I testified for him, and instead of serving time, Tupac was sentenced to do a fundraising concert for us. (The judge was so moved by what we were doing at APCH that he joined our board!) At a huge Mother's Day bash that Suge Knight, of Death Row Records, threw for all of his performers, Gideon and I felt like VIPs as we were ushered past burly bodyguards and seated at a table with Tupac and his mother, Afeni. They were thrilled to see me; I had helped Tupac stay out of jail. (Tupac was killed shortly before the concert could happen, a victim of the violent culture we are working so hard to protect the children from.)

Our music program took a giant step forward when Suge Knight provided the resources and equipment for us to build a full-size professional music and recording studio. Recording artist Flesh-n-Bone also contributed, donating high-quality studio microphones for our young musicians.

I became friends with Afeni Shakur, and through her I met actress Jasmine Guy. When Afeni brought Jasmine to see APCH, we had just leased the new building. As we walked from room to room, Jasmine's eyes lit up and she said, "I'll have the whole building painted inside and out." And she did. When that was done, she said, "You need a dance studio, you need mirrors, you need a barre, you need this and that." And I kept saying fine, fine. So Jasmine built a dance studio for us.

Then she put together a dance program and started teaching, an unbelievable dream-come-true opportunity for our aspiring young dancers. Jasmine brought in her sister, Monica Guy, and Monica got more and more involved with APCH. Now Monica runs the dance program with a loving but firm hand while Jasmine continues to be a tremendous supporter, dance teacher and a wonderful friend.

Our programs proved successful, and A Place Called Home gained recognition, both locally and nationally. We won more awards. Our children graduated, earned scholarships and got jobs. Our devoted circle of generous and visionary donors gradually expanded. Companies and volunteer organizations stepped up to participate alongside our staff.

And our staff evolved, too.

Among our regular visitors were priests, rabbis, imams, monks and nuns from many different orders, drawn to APCH because of the unusual harmony found between the Latino and African-American children—something that was not happening on the streets or in the schools. Security would ring me and say, "Rabbi Jan is here," or "Sister May is here." They came from all over the world. I would give them tours and information about APCH, offer them cookies and milk, and send them on their way.

Then, like the flying nun, Sister Pat dropped in. Returning from Rome, where she had been General Superior of the Religious of the Sacred Heart of Mary, Sister Patricia Connor had met the nun who would be taking her place in Rome and was handed a packet of papers describing APCH and the prophetic words, "This place is for you."

Sister Pat started as a part-time volunteer tutor at A Place Called Home in 1997. It wasn't long before I found a need for her wealth of teaching and administrative skills and hired her full-time. For seven years, strong and calming, she was central to all of the activities and decisions made at APCH. In 2003, when she was asked by her congregation to work as Provincial Superior of the Western American Province, Sister Pat had to leave our staff—a huge loss. But she would never abandon APCH; she's still a staunch board member, spiritual support and a treasured friend.

And then there's Christopher Smart. Chris grew up without much in the way of positive influence and started using drugs and alcohol at an early age. In high school, Chris played basketball and hoped that sports might be his ticket to success, but after he was injured in his senior year, things went from bad to worse. Even four years in the Marine Corps didn't help: he emerged with no practical skills and a serious substance abuse problem. He spent some time in vocational school and landed a job at General Motors, until the layoffs came.

So Chris headed west from Flint, Michigan, thinking California was the land of milk and honey for addicts. Not exactly. At twenty-nine, he found himself on skid row, where he lived—on the street—for two years. Finally, enough was enough and Chris got himself into a recovery program with the Los Angeles Mission. Once he was clean and ready to work again, he found his way to APCH through a friend, came in for an interview and I hired him immediately as a program assistant. Today, eight years later, Chris Smart works at APCH full-time as vice president of programs and is enrolled in a master's program in psychology.

Where other employers might find someone with Chris' background undesirable, I have found that personal experience with substance abuse, gangs and prison gives our staff powerful empathy for the children. That's not to say that prior misconduct is a prerequisite for employment, only that it's not an automatic reason for rejection. In a child's face, these staff members see a younger version of themselves. That vision fuels their passion to help.

There's always a feeling of warmth and good humor around A Place Called Home. Chris calls me his wife and I call him my husband. He walks into the development office and calls out, "Your husband is here!" We are family, all there for each other; it's part of the magic.

One day, while some of our APCH gang members were doing community service by painting the house adjacent to our parking lot, there was a drive-by shooting. As he climbed the ladder with his brush and paint can to finish the front wall of the house, Angelo was shot. Everyone shouted for me to come quick. With Sister Pat close behind me, I ran to Angelo, dropped to my knees and applied pressure to his stomach with my hands, trying to stop the gushing of his blood. The police showed up and shouted at me to step away from Angelo: I was interfering with a crime scene. I refused to move. Monique, Lawrence, some of my staff and a few of the older children—maybe twenty people all together (and potentially an unruly mob in the officers' eyes)—came out to see what was happening and were shoved against the wall, hands behind their heads. After the ambulance came and the paramedics took over my position at Angelo's side, we all moved back in to the safety of APCH, where our counselors did an impromptu debriefing.

Another time, the police department's gang intervention unit came into the APCH parking lot and began pushing some of our gang members up against the outside fence and the entryway walls. Sister Pat and I came running, shouting at them to stop hurting our children. They told us not to interfere or we would be arrested, and directed us to get into the back of the police car until things calmed down. Members and staff watched wide-eyed and slack-jawed as their founder and their program director, the nun, sat it out; they loved it. The police believed that one of our children had committed a crime. They took a few of the gang members in for questioning, but later released them.

Over time, our communication with the local police improved. Beat officers, local captains and Chief Bratton made friendly visits to APCH. They saw the value of what we were doing and even welcomed us into a room at the police station for our monthly board meetings.

Like the children, I had struggled with my lifelong Stupid label. I had been thrown out of school and many of our troubled teenagers and gang members had, too. I wanted them to succeed where I hadn't—to be able to finish high school and get a diploma or equivalency certificate at APCH. So we established an alliance with the Los Angeles Unified School District.

Whatever people donate to APCH gets plowed right back into our programs and into the community. Besides serving three meals a day, twice a week we open our patio to long lines of mothers who come to pick up sacks of fresh fruits, vegetables and bread. They carefully sort through donated books, clothes and furniture, taking home whatever they need.

By 2000, our membership had grown from 12 to 3,000. Every room in our building was overcrowded and serving multiple roles. I had found an even better use for closets: with the addition of a window and a phone line, they could be transformed into offices. We entertained grand visions of a true community center, a place with larger spaces where we could expand our already over-enrolled programs. We initiated a capital campaign to buy a building that would allow us to quadruple our space.

I called Johnny Carson, who had been such a strong supporter. He was concerned that the project would take the focus off the children, and he advised us to be cautious as we moved forward, emphasizing that if we were able to help just one child, that would be success enough for his money. When the building plans were ready, a year and a half later, I dropped them off at his office. He came down to APCH, everybody got to meet him, he got to see some of the results of his year-after-year donations and saw that we really did need the additional space. As he left he said, "I'm going to put a check in the mail for a million dollars." He did. Beyond gratitude, we were suddenly able to see our dreams materializing.

Then came the tragedy of September 11, 2001. Donation levels plunged. We were forced to abandon our expansion plans, reduce our staff and eliminate every bit of so-called excess from our budget.

But the children kept coming, and we kept serving them snacks, helping them with their homework, teaching them dance and music, counseling them through their emotional challenges, cheering their accomplishments in sports, art and academics, and as always, encouraging their dreams and promoting their self-esteem.

As I write this, we've learned to do more with less and are extremely grateful to see renewed generosity from our donors. In September 2003, as we celebrated our tenth anniversary, our membership stood at 3,800. Our young dancers gave a rousing performance to inaugurate our fully refurbished dance studio, a gift of the Footlighters (a philanthropic organization of women in theater) and a truly hopeful landmark for the years ahead.

No matter what we do, we can't shield the children entirely from the realities of the street. We've lost some children to gang violence, drugs and drive-by shootings. But we have also witnessed great change: drug-dealing gangsters turning into professional musicians, high-school dropouts earning scholarships to college, scrawny children turning into graceful dancers.

In ten years, many of our original members have entered adulthood. A whole new generation of children comes through our doors. From the earliest days, my vision for A Place Called Home has been fueled by hope and dreams, inspired by the heroic lives of our young members and challenged by the economics of survival in an uncertain world.

As I recently realized, my inspiration had had another

source as well. Mother's parents, Frances and Irving, gave me respite and helped me through some of the most difficult passages of my young life. But beyond that, they gave me access to the world of movies. If they were living in a rarefied world of the "rich and famous," the Mirisch brothers were also hardworking, creative masterminds who had strong principles. This all came back to me in 2002 as I watched the Academy Awards. There was my Great Uncle Walter handing an award to Sidney Poitier. In his acceptance speech, Mr. Poitier acknowledged some of the visionary people who had made his career possible, including "the Mirisch brothers, especially Walter, whose friendship lies at the very heart of this moment."

In the past, I had enjoyed the flash and fanfare of the Oscars. But as I listened to Sidney Poitier's inspiring words, I was suddenly crying.

As I thought about it, I realized that somehow, in spite of all the difficult and confusing messages of my youth, I had learned something from watching my grandfather and my great uncles. They didn't set out to teach me, but through their actions they *showed* me that all people are important and deserving of dignity and respect. They acted on their belief that intelligence, beauty and talent are not restricted or defined by skin color. They invested their time and money in that belief, without regard to those who would discourage them.

Almost every day, people ask me why I'm doing what I'm doing, why I would give up a lucrative job to spend my days and all my hopes in South Central Los Angeles.

And now I see that I was leaving out one of the most important reasons of all: the role modeling—the mentoring—of my uncles all those years ago.

The exposure to the world of entertainment and the people who create it had a lasting influence in another way. It allowed me to see that people, wherever they live, whatever their work, however great their fame, are just people. (Well . . . there was one exception. One day when I was a teenager, I was riding the elevator at my uncles' studio. The doors opened and Elvis Presley stepped in. I nearly fainted.)

It isn't his money or his fame that makes Johnny Carson an APCH angel. It's his vision, his honesty and his consistent commitment to act on what he believes. It isn't her grace or beauty that makes Jasmine Guy my friend. It's her soul-melting warmth and the expression on her face as she's teaching a dance class—an expression that says to a child who's all knees and elbows, you are a dancer, you're beautiful, you can do anything you want to do.

It's people's actions that make them stars and heroes in my mind. It doesn't matter if they've been in movies or in prison, they can walk through the doors of A Place Called Home and feel welcome. In spite of our challenges and our limitations, APCH has survived. The dreams are still alive.

A GANG OF MY OWN

More than anyone else, it was the gangbangers who really touched my heart. I'd look at these kids in their baggy pants, draped with chains, with their shaved heads and tattoos and weapons, and what I'd see was the light of god in their eyes. Behind their costumes and surly attitudes were children—eager to please, hungry for affection and trapped by the habits of their culture and the pressures of the street.

I knew something about habits, and I understood what it meant to be stuck with a label. Practically from birth, these kids struggle with labels that are reinforced on the street, in school, by the community and in their families: Bad, Failure, Hopeless, Criminal. They are throwaway children. Fifteen-, sixteen-, and seventeen-year-olds have no way to envision a real future; they can't imagine living beyond age twenty-one.

Just as I had turned to the juvenile delinquents when I

was an unhappy child, these children turn to the one place they know they can find support: gangs. Among their gang brothers and sisters they're accepted, even rewarded, for their attitudes and behavior. No one berates them, belittles them or turns them away.

But the price is steep. Within their gangs, the children learn to hate, to carry and use weapons, to use and sell drugs, to deface property and to bury everything soft, trusting and childlike in themselves. They're always watching their backs, and if they manage to dodge the bullets, they carry with them the continual stress of fear and the lasting trauma of seeing their friends and family members die—sometimes right in front of them.

I've always been passionate about the underdog; even as a little kid I gave away my Christmas presents to needy children. By the time I met the gangbangers, I had learned that change is possible. I had navigated the rapids of my sobriety, and I believed that if the gang members wanted to change, they could, too, one day at a time. I would do everything I could to assist them. I'd help them find jobs—even if it meant hiring them myself. I'd help them get counseling, get into A.A. and get back into school. I'd give the children my money, clothes, shoes, food—whatever they needed. I'd never throw anybody away.

And if they slipped and ended up back in jail, well then, we'd just start back at day one again. I'd say, you call me from jail. When they did, I'd say, I want you to go to church; are you going to classes? Are you going to A.A. meetings? And I'd tell them, when you get out, you come back to A Place Called Home. No matter how many times they slipped, they knew that I wouldn't abandon them. As long as they stayed alive, there would always be another chance.

Nothing that the children do upsets me, because I know it's natural. A child will say, "I didn't have the gun," and I know it's exactly what I would have said when confronted with authority. Like many children who are abused, I was scared to tell the truth, so I lied. I wasn't trying to get away with something; it wasn't that conscious. Even now, if you ask me a surprise question, I'll pop out an answer instantly. It's not necessarily the truth, but it's an answer. The truth requires listening and trust.

The children came into my office, and I'd pay attention to them, ask them what do you want to do, what do you like, tell me the truth and I'll listen. In their lives, nobody listens to them. Nobody sees them as individuals; they're always lumped together with all the other "bad" kids. Even their parents are afraid of them. But I wasn't afraid; I saw them as children with dangerous toys.

One day one of my staff members came to me, indignant, and said, "Julio is stealing food. I saw him take food from the kitchen." I said, "Okay, here's what I want you to do. I want you go back there and pack up four more bags of groceries for him to take home." Things like that aren't done out of greed, they're done out of need. If he's hungry, there are probably hungry people at home, too. We had food and they didn't. The solution just didn't seem complicated to me.

When we moved out of the church into our new building, we moved into a neighborhood in which almost every wall, fence and stop sign was "tagged" with graffiti. Our building was a huge white block of stucco with the APCH name and logo near the top, a tempting blank slate for "taggers." From the day we opened, I noticed that there was a teenager in gang colors riding his bike around the center, along the street, up and down the alley. I learned that his name was Benito, and that he was a hard-core gang member and head of one of the local gangs. I was trying to figure out what he was doing, so one day I stopped him. He said he was watching me. What for? I asked. He said that he was watching over the center to make sure it didn't get tagged.

He cruised the street on his bike, never asking for anything and never setting foot inside, but sometimes, as I pulled out of the driveway in my Jeep, he'd tell me to put on my seat belt. I couldn't believe it; he's telling *me* to be careful. This went on for a while. Benito got shot a few times, went to jail and eventually showed up again. One day as he was standing outside, I began to talk with him. He told me he needed a job. I knew that my staff would be furious—nobody shared my faith in these gang kids—but I said, okay, I'll hire you, but if you're going to work here, you have to sign our pledge, go to school, get into a twelve-step program and start going to counseling. He did. Then, one by one, his friends started coming in. I hired them, too. Nobody could believe it. Benito led, they followed. They were ready for change. That's what made me roll up my sleeves.

These tough young thugs began to look at me as their mother. They actually used that word. They were huge and mean-looking to everyone else, but they'd come into my office, sit on my lap and want hugs, like three-year-olds. They shared their problems; I offered solutions. They trusted me, told me their sad and frightening stories, and never questioned that my suggestions were right for them. They knew that I believed in them, that I wasn't afraid of them and that I would never hurt them. I protected them, and they protected me.

If I heard that there was a big gang fight brewing, I'd find them and say, you may as well just check yourself into jail. I'd tell them they'd end up dead. They didn't care; they felt invincible. Sometimes I'd go looking for them in my car if I knew that they were in trouble. I'd drive through the neighborhood, pull up in front of their house and say, what are you doing? Why are you hanging out? Go inside. Go do your homework. And because I listened to them, they'd listen to me.

I talked to their parole officers, appeared in court for them and even arranged for a funeral if the family couldn't afford one. It's horrible to go to a child's funeral. There, all alone, are the parents of the dead child. The neighbors and friends, aunts and uncles, all stayed away. The gangs made it too dangerous; a funeral could turn into a battlefield. I had buried too many of the children. That's when I knew we had to do something to empower the mothers, too, and created Mothers Against Violence.

Mothers Against Violence came together because their

children were dying on the streets of Los Angeles. They needed their own safe place to go with their fears, and to feel that, in dealing with their children, they were not alone. They needed their own gang. We set up meetings and offered health and cooking classes. Suddenly these women had someone to talk to. Instead of locking their doors in fear and isolation, they now have a lifeline. When there's trouble, they support each other. And they know that, for at least a few hours each day, their children are safe here. A Place Called Home is an island of safety in the middle of a war zone. When I announced that I was forming this new group, the women came running up to me, hugging and kissing me, and signing up. They're always blessing me, thanking me. They call me their angel, the Mother Teresa of South Central.

I gathered support from wherever I could find it. One of our gangbangers, Eddie, had been a member of APCH for a couple of years. He got shot, and the bullet lodged next to his heart, too close to remove. I visited him in the hospital with some of the other staff members and kids. We were frightened. We didn't want to lose another child. The Agape International Spiritual Center was honoring me with an anti-violence award the following weekend, so I brought a bunch of the gang members and some of the mothers to the ceremony. I went up to receive my award, told Eddie's story and watched as eight hundred people joined hands in prayer. He's still walking around with his bullet.

One of my strongest allies in this gang intervention

work is Chico Brown, the APCH director of gang prevention and intervention. I got a call one day from Robert Greenwald, a movie producer and member of our board, saying that he had met a young man who might be an asset to APCH. Chico came in to meet me. Within minutes, I asked him to join my staff. I was drawn to him immediately and knew it was important for him to be a part of A Place Called Home. He told me he was in a halfway house and tried to tell me more, but I stopped him; that didn't matter to me. I asked him if he could do gang prevention. "Right up my alley," he said.

So I hired him, and I was right. He was perfect. He knew exactly how to talk with the children, how to gain their confidence and respect, and what to tell them that would really make a difference in their lives. It wasn't until much later that I let Chico tell me his story.

Leroy "Chico" Brown was raised in Compton, California, in what he described as a pretty decent family. But he started gangbanging early, got shot when he was twelve, and watched his best friend die in his arms when he was just fourteen. The violence continued, but somehow Chico managed to graduate from high school and went on to a profitable career selling street drugs.

In 1990, he was indicted on federal charges of distribution of cocaine, went to jail and spent a year fighting his case, which he won. But once he was out, he got right back into the business, this time on a much larger scale. Now he was selling crack cocaine with "Freeway" Rick Ross, who had an unlimited supply. Chico was making a lot of money, shopping on Rodeo Drive and feeling like a rich young guy from Compton. When they were finally busted, the story unfolded in the papers, on television and in a book, *Dark Alliance*, by Gary Webb, a reporter from the *San Jose Mercury-News*. Chico had been a player in a huge, complex web of intrigue and drugs that involved smugglers, bureaucrats, the CIA, the U.S. Drug Enforcement Agency, the Nicaraguan Contras and Oliver North.

Chico was sentenced to ten years in prison. There he looked around and saw young men—kids, really—facing sentences of thirty to forty years, who had been sent up for possession on a third strike. He started talking with these kids about gangs and drugs. He conducted classes. After about five years, the prison officials realized that the work he was doing was making a difference, so they let him out to speak at various juvenile halls. Chico could see that *his* life was changing, too.

He eventually served seven and a half years, including a year in solitary. About the time he was being released, he got a call from Robert Greenwald, who had purchased the movie rights to *Dark Alliance*. In their conversations, Chico talked about his interest in eventually opening up a youth center where he could continue the work he had started in prison. Robert told him about A Place Called Home. When Chico walked in the door that day, APCH was exactly the place he had envisioned.

Chico was released from prison on September 29, 2001, and started working at APCH on October 7. Like the other gang members, he talks to me as if I'm his mother. He calls me Mom and refers to himself as my son. I listen, and he pays attention.

Chico spends his days at APCH giving back everything he learned the hard way. He says that he wants the kids to know the truth so they can't say that they didn't know. He runs a six-month course for boys and girls ages thirteen to twenty. They meet two evenings a week to talk about what their actions mean, and how those actions can affect their lives. Plus, he takes them on field trips for a little reality check: to prisons, to the intensive-care unit at the county hospital and to the morgue. He also makes sure they see the up-side of staying clean. He takes them to sporting events, introduces them to top personalities in sports and entertainment, and works with neighborhood corporations to make sure that when the kids are ready to work, they will have jobs waiting for them. Whatever happens, when they need to talk, they know that Chico is always just a phone call away.

We are helping the children to expand their vision, to see that they have options. In addition to gang prevention and intervention, counseling helps them begin to learn that they are not locked in to their labels and habits. It's a tough road, but if they want to make a change, there are choices available to them. We help them learn about who they are and what they want so that the choices make sense to them. We let them know that they do not have to do this alone. They can choose whether to stay home, stand on a street corner and get shot, cruise for trouble, or come in to APCH, go to school, get a job and maybe live past twenty-one. Suddenly, they see the possibility of having their own family, a house, even a safe neighborhood to live in. If they can make that change, they're no longer passing down the generational baton of violence. Instead of flashing a gang sign, they can flash a peace sign. Maybe they can be different. Those are real choices and a huge change: to know that, at least in one place, it is safe to imagine a different life. It's A Place Called Home.

DIANA

It had never occurred to me that my life could turn so dramatically on chance encounters in a coffee shop, but it has happened twice. The first time, a perfect stranger helped me to get tax-exempt status and come up with a name for my new youth center. The next time, several years later, a woman at the next table hears me talking about closets and interrupts to ask if I know a "good closet person." Outside, when we spoke again, we were very surprised to discover that we already had a connection—through A Place Called Home! That woman was Diana.

At the time we met, I was still recovering from my painful relationship with Lewis. I had thrown myself into work, A.A., yoga and, as always, dieting. The day Diana and I met, I was going to my first Overeaters Anonymous (O.A.) meeting. She had been in O.A. for a while and was interested in learning more about the tougher A.A. rules.

So in addition to Diana already knowing about A Place Called Home and being involved as a donor, we had this shared commitment to making ourselves better. It was an instant friendship. Over the coming months, we talked on the phone, had coffee together and met for breakfast; I went to O.A. with her and she went to A.A. with me. We went to O.A. conventions and A.A. retreats. She worked out with me at Gold's Gym. I shared with her the personal inventory I was doing with my A.A. sponsor, Clancy, and helped her as she began her fourth-step inventory for O.A.

Diana was a wonderful breath of fresh air in my life. I invited her down to see what we were doing at A Place Called Home, and she loved it from the first minute. We joined a writing class together, and I wrote three stories that turned into chapters in this book. That led us into journal writing, following the steps in Julia Cameron's book, *The Artist's Way.*

No matter what we were doing, we always laughed a lot. Diana is very, very funny, but for some reason it appeared to be the world's best-kept secret. Her family and friends seemed to see her as this orderly, serious person. But we felt so at ease with each other that we could be serious *and* silly. I hadn't ever been that soulfully connected with anyone.

I was living in a little apartment in Venice, and Diana had just moved into a home in Santa Monica. She invited me over to see the house and meet her husband of thirty years. I was envious of her beautiful large closets. We walked along the beach or on the bluff overlooking the ocean, back and forth between her house and mine. We even leased a little apartment that we could use as an office. We were going to write this book.

Diana helped me sort out the rage and confusion I felt over my relationship with Lewis and went with me to the pretrial meeting with the forensic psychiatrist and, later, to the trial.

We wrote together and talked endlessly. I got to know Diana's daughters, and she got to know Gideon. I had always hated to travel, but with Diana, leaving home wasn't frightening, it was *fun*. We went on spiritual retreats to Ojai, California, several times. We were such good friends.

We both loved to shop, and wherever we were, we would go in and out of stores and find wonderful treasures. One day we had gone into this store in Beverly Hills called *Girlfriends,* and we bought two hats that said GIRL-FRIENDS. The next day we put them on and met Gideon for breakfast. He started laughing and said, "Do you know what that suggests?" Diana and I said no. We had no idea. So that's how our relationship went for several years.

Eventually Diana invited me to move into the guest cottage behind her house, so I gave up my apartment. I had some minor surgery, and she nursed me through my recovery. She was a great nurse. We had fun and laughed and wrote and went to meetings. When she and her husband separated, I was there to support her emotionally, just as she had supported me.

How our relationship changed, I don't know, but one day it did, to our mutual surprise. We hadn't even talked about it, but suddenly, easily, we started an intimate relationship. I adored Diana. She was the dearest friend I had ever had, and I had fallen in love with her. I had never felt so safe.

I moved from the guest cottage into the main house. We tried to be discreet, but everyone seemed to know what was going on. Our children were talking about us behind our backs. Even Diana's brother and sister-in-law knew before we told them. We were the last ones to find out. As Gideon says, it's the best thing that ever could have happened to me.

This absolutely was not in my life plan, but Diana is the kindest, most loving, most generous, funniest, smartest human being I have ever known. Together, we have enriched our lives and brightened the lives of everyone around us.

My life had turned another corner.

Then we had the accident.

CRASH

On the evening of Sunday, May 23, 1999, I was driving Diana home from downtown Los Angeles in my new green Jeep Cherokee. We left the play at the Mark Taper Forum a little early, got on the Santa Monica Freeway, headed west and took the 5th Street exit. That's all I remember. The details come from Diana.

In front of numerous witnesses, a motorcycle going sixty miles an hour went through a red light and slammed straight into my door. He came crashing through the driver's-side window, and his helmet collided with my head. The Jeep rolled all the way over and righted itself. Everybody was screaming, "Stop the car, stop the car," and finally someone reached in and switched off the ignition. Diana, who was rattled and bruised but essentially okay, called to me. I didn't respond. Looking beyond the twisted gearshift, all she could see was my butt, my legs and my bare feet. From the hips up, my body was hanging all the way out the window. My seat belt hadn't held me. My shoes had disappeared, ripped away in the crash.

As soon as the car stopped moving, three men ran over, lifted me out and laid me down on the ground. By the time Diana walked around the car moments later, there was a huge pool of dark red blood running along the pavement under and around me. My eyes were rolled back in my head, and I was breathing in a terrible sort of death rattle.

If there was one bit of good fortune in this event, it was that the crash happened just two blocks from a fire station, and the paramedics arrived within five minutes. They cut open my shirt, hooked me up to monitors, covered me with a blanket and, Diana recalls, kept saying, "Stay with us, Debrah. Stay with us."

Lifting me into the ambulance, they told Diana that she couldn't ride with me; I might not make it to the hospital. In a panic, Diana followed in the emergency paramedic truck, and sirens blaring, the two vehicles raced across town to the Trauma Center in the Emergency Room at UCLA.

By the time Diana ran into the E.R., I was already wired up to monitors. They did X-rays and M.R.I.s of my entire body and determined that I had a broken clavicle, broken ribs, a great deal of internal and external battering, and one of my lungs had been punctured. I had a concussion, a very serious scalp wound and who knew what kind of injury to my brain. A giant gash in the back of my head had caused the profuse bleeding.

(The motorcyclist was unhurt. Like a good drunk, he

walked out of the hospital on his own power the next morning. His blood test was lost; he was never charged with anything and never even got a ticket.)

I regained a small measure of consciousness in the E.R.—not enough to talk or respond, and I certainly wasn't aware, but the doctors determined that I was not in a deep coma. My eyes were open, but nobody was home. Once I was stabilized, they moved me from Emergency into the Neurological Intensive Care Unit. Diana never left my side.

She hired a private respiratory therapist to assist her in watching over me and rallied the forces, who sat anxiously in the waiting room hoping for some good news. Along with Mother, my sisters Wendy (who had immediately flown in from New York) and Victoria, Gideon, Monique and Sister Pat, Diana's children and friends came to support us, as well as her ex-husband and his wife-to-be, my cousins and my closest friends. Arianna Huffington made the first phone call to the I.C.U. Everybody was there, but I have no memory of anyone.

A ventilator breathed for me, and a maze of tubes pumped food and drugs into my system and waste products out. Not much happened on Monday. On Tuesday or Wednesday it appeared that I was watching the people in the room. When I looked blankly at Diana, she said to Victoria, "She doesn't know me." Through the fog, and around the obstruction of the breathing tube, I managed to communicate a gruntlike, "Are you nuts?" It was at this point that they realized that I was still Deb. Diana handed me a small clipboard and a pencil and I scrawled, "Get me out of here."

My condition wavered. When a neurologist came to check on me and encouraged me to cough, I tried to rip out all the tubes. I had a track record as a bad patient, and I immediately started living up to my reputation.

With focused determination, Diana turned my I.C.U. room into a fortress of security and healing. She policed my visitors and made sure that every square inch of visible wall space was covered with the colorful drawings, cards and letters I was getting from the children at A Place Called Home. Enlarging photographs of the people (and animals) I loved, she pinned them to the bulletin board. She read loving messages to me and played tapes of special music to stimulate healing brain waves. If my condition was fragile, my room was a celebration of life; nurses from all over the hospital paraded through to see what was going on. They had never seen anything quite like it, certainly not in the somber atmosphere of the Neuro I.C.U. Diana's son-in-law, Chris, and Gideon shared overnight duties so Diana could get a few hours of sleep.

On Thursday, I took a turn for the worse. My family and friends watched the attendant wheel me away for another M.R.I. When the attendant brought me back, the doctor announced that I had had a stroke and that my right side was paralyzed. I couldn't write. My right hand curled in on itself and lay lifeless at my side.

On Friday, I had a heart attack. Although I raised my left hand and flashed a peace sign as I was once again wheeled off, everyone thought that it was the end. The mood in the waiting room turned dark. I returned from my latest battery of tests, and one by one, people came in to talk to me, maybe to say good-bye. I was unaware.

My friend Judith made laminated tags that looked like back-stage passes for all of my visitors. Along with the APCH logo—the same image of dancing children that was tattooed on my wrist—the tags said "I ❤ Deb" in huge letters. In the waiting room, "Team Debrah"—my extended family of friends and relatives—stood in a circle and prayed, cried, and sang. In the waiting room was another group of people who had been sharing the long days, hoping for some sign of improvement, some miracle, from their wounded son, also a patient on the Neuro I.C.U. They, too, joined the circle to pray.

Specialists came and went: cardiologists, neurologists, pulmonologists. They could watch over me and give me endless tests, but nobody could predict the extent of the damage to my brain or the lingering effect on my heart. Would I be able to walk? Talk? Would I live? They couldn't say.

The care at UCLA, especially from my neurologist, was wonderful. But Diana, in addition, tapped into every resource she could find. It turned out that Sister Pat's brother, Stroud Connor, is a neurologist in Northern California, and he became the liaison between Diana and the UCLA neurologist to further decipher the tests, medical jargon and diagnoses. Diana called Helen, my psychic. Helen told her that I was fine, not experiencing any pain and that I wasn't going to die. This happened, she said, because I had to learn how to love myself the way I loved the children, how to turn it inward. Helen laughed and said, "It would have to be something this big to slow Debrah down."

Somehow, little by little, I began to recover. I couldn't talk, but I made eye contact, and Diana saw volumes in the movement of my eyebrows. Mostly I was angry. As sick as I was—and I had absolutely no idea how sick I was, for a long time—I wanted out of there. My spirit was intact.

When I threw a pillow at Sister Pat, everyone knew I had "returned."

Over the course of the next week, I regained some of the movement on my right side. But my condition was still precarious. The doctors wanted to keep me at UCLA, but Kaiser Permanente, my insurance carrier, wanted me moved to their facility. The night before I left, they turned off the ventilator. While Diana held her breath, I took one on my own.

After two weeks in Neuro I.C.U., I was loaded into an ambulance, and Diana, Victoria and Sister Pat followed me to Kaiser Permanente Medical Center. It was a depressing move, from the hub of medical science, with every possible doctor, nurse and machine available, to what felt like an empty bowling alley. The place echoed. There was nobody to meet us, my papers hadn't been transferred and there was no doctor to do the intake.

Eventually a nurse showed up and, following the instructions of my vigilant personal care team, got me into a bed. However, clearly this would not do. Diana called to see if I could be readmitted to UCLA, but my insurance wouldn't allow it. Wendy, concerned about the care I would get at the new facility, had put on her best research persona and within a few hours had found a skilled private nurse to attend to my needs. Then Diana got the name of a highly recommended internist at Kaiser who helped pull all the necessary strings to get me moved three days later. I had just started to speak and could give simple answers to the doctor's questions. Victoria and Diana coached me with the answers as though my life depended on it. It did. We didn't feel safe there.

This time I was relocated to a rehab facility. When I was settled in my new room, Diana, exhausted from nearly three weeks of unrelenting vigilance and anxiety, turned to leave for the night. I refused to let her go; she had to sleep with me, under the covers, in my tiny, single hospital bed.

When we woke up the next morning, I looked at my wrist and was suddenly aware, and very upset, that my favorite watch was gone, a casualty of the crash weeks before. Then, Diana tells me, I turned to her and said, "Oh, can you call Colin for me?" Here's Diana, absolutely drained from the emotional strain, not knowing whether I will even live, let alone be able to function, and I'm casually asking her to make a phone call for me. She said okay, she would call Colin (a member of the APCH board and a good friend), but she didn't know his number. I rattled it off. Diana, in shock, dialed the number, handed me the phone and I talked to Colin as if nothing unusual had happened. Then I wanted to call more people, reciting their numbers to Diana one after the other.

From that point forward, I regained a lot of my speech and motor skills, and became entirely focused on a single goal: going home. When I was admitted to rehab, the doctors had said that I would be there for three months. I still had no idea what had happened to me or why I was in this strange place, so I immediately launched my campaign to get myself out. I told Diana and anyone else who would listen that if they didn't let me go home, I'd call my gang members and they'd take me out bodily, like a jail-break. I continued to demand that Diana sleep with me, telling her that if she went home, I'd go home, too.

Everything became a battle. Doctors, nurses and therapists wanted to test me. I refused. They wanted to keep the rail up at the side of my bed. I refused. I was unable to understand or accept directions or to believe that there was anything wrong with me.

The second day in rehab, my yoga teacher, Max, came to visit. Diana left the room for five minutes, and when she came back, Max was gone and I was out of bed, starting to do a headstand.

My friends pushed me around the building in a wheel-chair, down to the gift shop and outside for my first breath of fresh air since the accident. I started doing some walking. I held court day and night. Monique was there. Benito came and held my hand. My massage therapist, Candace Veach, came and worked on my bruised and unused muscles. It hurt. Although Gideon was to sit at my side through the night, and Diana hired a nurse for overnight duty, hoping for a night in her own bed, I *still* made Diana sleep over.

A speech pathologist came in to start my rehab. I tried to send her away. Diana, who's a speech pathologist herself, begged me to work with this person for just five minutes. So we talk a bit, and she begins giving me word tests. Suddenly I'm eight years old and back in school, terrified and Stupid: I don't know the answers to her questions; my words are scrambled. Finally, Diana explained to the therapist that, even at my very best, I wouldn't be able to answer these questions, that I often mixed up my pronouns and used the wrong words. Diana promised to monitor my progress and hoped that, over the course of the coming months, my comprehension and word-finding problems would resolve themselves spontaneously.

Terribly worried, Diana tried to convince me that I should stay in rehab, but I was tenaciously focused on getting out. The occupational therapists told me that they would consider my release when I could walk up and down the steps, thinking they were challenging me with a long-term goal. By the next day I had mastered the stairs.

Ornery and contrary, I refused to cooperate. I looked blankly at everyone who tried patiently to explain to me what I had been through and the hazards of my rash behavior. Diana realized that, with my determination, nothing would ever be accomplished in rehab and, indeed, I had to go home. And if I went home, she could go home, too. She informed the staff. They told her my release was impossible, but that they would hold a meeting to discuss it.

The rehab facility had six representatives at the meeting—doctors, nurses and therapists. I had seventeen. "Team Debrah" turned out in force to support me. I told the rehab people that I wanted and needed to go home.

They said, we can't send you home yet because you need to be able to take a shower on your own, cook a meal, make your bed and so on. Then Diana said, no, she doesn't need to be able to do those things; I'll be assisting her, and we have full-time help in the house. Mother piped up, saying that maybe it would be *good* for me to stay in rehab for a while. I turned to her and barked, "Shut up!" I would tolerate no opposition. My therapists, doctors, friends, sister and son spoke up on my behalf.

Finally they said to Diana that the only way I could go home was if she arranged for round-the-clock nursing. Diana agreed and hired a nurse.

Instead of three months, I was released from rehab after just five days. We drove home. But not straight home. We made a little detour. Talking about a safe car, I told Diana to stop at the Volvo dealer. She said, "*Now?* Are you nuts?" We stopped. We bought a shiny red Volvo station wagon, left it on the lot for detailing and headed home.

Diana was nervous about the nurse, knowing that I wouldn't cooperate with her. When the housekeeper greeted us at the door, she told us that the nurse had been there, seen the cats and dogs, begun to sneeze and left. I got what I wanted: I was home safe with Diana.

SMART AS A BELL

Home at last, I was still far from healed. I had a broken collarbone that would have to knit together in its own good time; my broken ribs made every breath painful; I had a horrible head wound (and a large, bristly shaved patch) that had to be cleaned and dressed regularly; I was still recovering from deep bruises; I had significant brain injury; and, although I was awake and talking, I had no recollection of the accident or most of the intervening weeks of my touch-and-go recovery.

I thought I should be able to resume my normal activities. I missed the children, hated being away from work and yoga, and was "ready" to go to the gym, ride my bike and Rollerblade. I became a bratty teenager, testing Diana's affection and the patience of just about everybody else.

Diana immediately found me a wonderful physical therapist. It was only when Sherry started to work on me that she discovered a deep, painful indentation in the muscle below my left shoulder, and we figured out that the car must have run over my arm as it rolled. Nobody had noticed it while I was hospitalized.

I began to see a cranial-sacral therapist who worked to heal my brain, body and spirit. She would say, "Debrah, you walked into this room, and you know who's in the room with you? This room is filled with angels." She called on a pantheon of spiritual superstars to help me recover.

I continued a regular round of appointments and tests with all of my doctors, who were amazed at my progress. My psychotherapist, Sharon Gedan, helped me begin to examine my turbulent emotions churned up by the trauma.

My massage therapist worked on me at the house. My yoga teachers came to visit, and I caused Diana palpitations as I again threatened to stand on my head or do "Downward Dog." Arianna had visited me at the hospital, and when I got home she brought over her mother and an amazing Greek dinner they had cooked for me.

My thick skull had saved me during the accident, but it also made it hard for me to understand my limitations. Because of my stroke in the hospital, I was taking Coumadin, a blood thinner; if I fell or cut myself, I could bleed to death, internally or externally. But that didn't stop me from strapping on my Rollerblades one day when Diana left the house. I didn't fall that time, but months later, when I convinced Diana to go bike riding, I fell off the bike two blocks from the house. That was the end of that.

The doctors told me I couldn't go back to work for eighteen months. Five months after the accident, I returned to A Place Called Home, driving myself back and forth each day for a few hours with the children. There was no way that anyone could stop me. On one of my first days back, a photographer arrived from *Newsweek* to take the picture that would accompany the "My Turn" article I had submitted shortly before the accident. I was surprised to see myself looking like such a mess. In the photo, my mouth is smiling, but my hair looks flat and lifeless and so do my eyes. I still had no idea how damaged I was.

One day, three years after the accident, Gideon was driving me home from Victoria's house (which Jasmine Guy was using as a location in the film she was making about her life) when I began to slur and drool. Gideon said, "Mom, what's the problem?" I said, "I'm fine." He took me home and we called the neurologist, Dr. Shimizu. I went to see him, and he told me that I had had another small stroke. Diana was in New York for a conference, so I flew there to meet her. She and our two dear friends, Beryl and Gail, also speech pathologists, noticed that I seemed tired, was less able to focus and was having more word-finding problems than normal.

For the first time, I began to feel slightly discouraged. But I continued with my life, going to work, going to the gym and spending time with the people I loved. In June 2003, on my way to exercise one day, I decided I wanted to have a cappuccino with Gideon, who lived nearby. I called him, parked and jumped out of the car. I was thinking that I should probably change into my workout shoes, but I felt too rushed. I started across the street in my sparkly red, three-inch platform backless sandals. I was running to make the light and went flying, crashing hard onto the pavement. Gideon looked me over and determined that I hadn't broken any bones; I had scraped and bruised my hands and knees. He cautioned me about wearing open shoes. We had our coffee, and I drove home. A little while later, I was standing in my living room when I got very dizzy. My left eye started flickering like a strobe, and then I lost the sight entirely for thirty seconds or more. The side of my face was numb. I found Diana and she called Dr. Shimizu, who sent me to the Emergency Room.

They took me in and hooked me up. A few hours later, I began to feel a little better, but I also felt strange. I told Diana that I thought I was going to die. It was the beginning of a new level of awareness of my own vulnerability.

The doctors wanted to keep me overnight. I didn't want to stay, but I did. They ran all the usual tests, but Dr. Shimizu couldn't see anything concrete. He still wasn't sure exactly what had happened; my symptoms were very similar to the onset of migraine. But because of my history, he decided we needed to look further.

He sent me for another M.R.I. One of the residual effects of my original, paralyzing stroke was a 30-percent blockage of an artery in my brain. The result of this new

M.R.I. was sobering. The amount of constriction was now at 70 percent. Diana and I talked about the significance of this newest diagnosis: I was probably going to die, and soon.

Dr. Shimizu directed me to the head of brain surgery at UCLA who set an appointment for a more specific brain scan. "You have no blockage," this doctor said, looking at the test results. The narrowing of the originally damaged blood vessels seemed to have reversed itself. Listening to this new information, Diana and I were dumbfounded. How was it possible that my death sentence had been lifted within just two weeks? The 70-percent blockage reading was a false positive. So now I was going to live.

We had to figure out why I was continuing to have these small strokes. I went to see a hematologist at UCLA. He looked at my tests, and said I'd like to get you off Coumadin. I was so excited: no more weekly blood tests, no more stern warnings not to skate, not to fall, not to do a headstand. The doctor said, before we change your meds, let's make sure that you don't have a hole in your heart. I looked at him. *A hole in my heart?* It's possible, he said, that your strokes may be the result of blood clots traveling through an opening in your heart to your brain.

We were referred to someone who would do the necessary test. Searching for a heart defect used to require exploratory heart surgery, but today a test using a flexible probe and sound waves can be done in a doctor's office and the results known immediately. Diana took me to have the test done, and we sat in the treatment room.

Before the doctor could insert the probe, my throat needed to be numb, so he sprayed it with lidocaine and said he'd be back.

I had a seizure.

My arms and legs were flailing; my head was turning side to side, back and forth uncontrollably. Frantic, Diana called the nurse to get the doctor right away. He came back and explained with little apparent concern that I was having a reaction to the lidocaine. Diana said, can't you stop this? Isn't there some antidote? No, he said mildly, I would have to wait it out; it will stop in about fifteen minutes. He went back up to his office, leaving us alone in the room and telling the nurse to call him in fifteen minutes. Diana just held me, trying to calm me, not even daring to think what kind of further damage my poor brain was enduring.

By the time the doctor came back, my spasms had quieted, but I appeared to be unconscious. He said, "Debrah, can you hear me?" I opened my eyes and said yes. He talked to me enough that he thought I was lucid, and I followed his directions. He inserted the probe, and began to navigate the terrain of my heart. "Looks normal so far," he said. Our spirits fell. We didn't want normal, we wanted a hole, which would explain my recurring strokes. But just before he was finished, the doctor saw two little bubbles move between the chambers of my heart. He pointed to the monitor, and Diana saw them, too. A hole. We were elated.

It's called a patent foramen ovale, an opening that was

supposed to close at birth, but didn't. Finally, a reason for the strokes. The next step was to find someone to repair it.

After the test, I was a mess. I had been plunged into the darkest time of my life. Nothing—not abuse or cancer or even the accident itself—had been as horrible as my reaction to the lidocaine. During my seizure, I heard voices repeating "One two one two," over and over, obsessively, a circular one-track recording in my brain that I could not stop. I felt like I was stuck in madness with no escape. Plus, the doctors now told me that I could not work anymore. It sounded like a death sentence. I thought, *How can they not know that I am someone who can keep working, no matter what?*

I was without hope, convinced I was dying. The seizure jolted not just my body and my mind, but my memory. Buried feelings and reactions to the crash—and to my other traumas—came surging to the surface, dèjá vu. I had successfully dissociated my mind from my body during the abuse by my father, husband and boyfriend, and during my cancer and alcoholism; it became obvious that I had done the same thing after the accident. Suddenly there was no way to distract myself from the feelings and memories—no booze, no one to beat me up. Just me. I was shaken into consciousness.

All this was happening just as I started writing this book. For the first time, I was willing to look at the truth. Feelings of guilt, sadness, anger, frustration and helplessness surfaced. I had been hurt; I had hurt others. As I began to tell the story, I slowly found words to describe my feelings. (This process continues. Every day I am crushed by pounding waves of rage, regret, and empathy. But now, instead of hiding from them or turning them back on myself, I am connecting these emotions with the right people and circumstances in my past. I thought quitting smoking was the hardest thing I'd ever done; now I've discovered something even harder.)

We found a doctor who could do the heart repair. On September 22, 2003, Dr. Sibel Kar inserted a slender catheter through a tiny incision in my groin, feeding it into my heart and clipping together the torn edges of the hole. He repaired what he called a "sizeable" hole, and I stayed overnight in the hospital. Almost immediately, I experienced a huge increase in my energy level. But it wasn't until the beginning of 2004 that the depression and anxiety subsided, and I really felt like myself for the first time since the accident.

With the unbelievable patience and insight of my doctors, my therapist, my family, my friends and my Diana, I made my way back. Six days after my heart was patched, Dr. Kar, Dr. Judelson (my cardiologist) and her assistant, Charlie, and Sharon Gedan attended the tenth anniversary fundraising gala for A Place Called Home. I felt doubly lucky: I was alive to celebrate this milestone, and I had my miracle workers at my side.

The accident probably saved my life. My father and my uncle both died of heart disease at a very young age, and if the accident hadn't happened, I might never have had all these tests and found the flaw in my heart. Today, although we are still sorting out a few issues, the doctors say that my heart is strong, and there is no trace of the heart attack.

As someone who needs to win, to be strong and to persevere in the face of any adversity, it has been nearly impossible for me to recognize my own limitations. Every instinct drives me to deny any frailty; rather, my impulse is always to ignore my body's signals and to push myself even harder.

Nearly five years from the date of the accident, I am finally able to reflect on Helen's words to Diana: that the message that I needed to learn was how to love myself the way I loved the children. Part of learning to love myself has been to acknowledge that I am not invincible, and I will survive only if I take care of myself.

Now there's another kind of pain in my heart: the deep regret over all of the mistakes that I have made in my relationship with my son, Gideon.

GIDEON

Maybe, as they say, the first five years of a child's life are the formative ones. Otherwise how could this child of an abused alcoholic have turned into such a sweet, kind, generous, loving, smart man?

As Gideon was growing up, I thought that because I loved him more than life itself, I was being a good mother. But at each stage of my unfolding life, I've had a chance to reflect on the flaws in that notion. As I held Gideon and tried to reassure him before my cancer surgery, I saw a child who had already endured divorce, abrupt moves, a wild, drug-using mother and who was now facing the possible loss of that mother without a moment's preparation. Years later, once I got sober, I saw that alcohol had numbed me to the emotional needs of my child just as it had numbed me to my own feelings. I came to see that my dolls had had a better mother than Gideon; they had a sober mother. When I became a very focused and available foster mother to Monique and Lawrence, I began to see that, even sober, I had been preoccupied and unavailable to Gideon, rationalizing my absences with the importance of my commitments to work, A.A. and the men in my life.

And finally, through the painful medium of my accident, I have become aware of the bigger picture of my relationship with Gideon. Only now can we slowly begin to get to know each other, honestly, openly, as adults. That Gideon is willing, capable and forgiving enough to begin this process, is simple proof of what I have always believed: he is an angel.

Following the accident, after I got out of rehab, Diana invited Gideon to move into the guest cottage behind our house. It was part of her gift to me; she knew that nothing could make me happier than to have him nearby as I was recovering. So we began our relationship anew. For the four years that he lived there, I got to see him almost every day, to share his life with him and to let him be a participant in the slow restoration of my mental and physical health. We had coffee together every morning, laughed, argued, compromised, shared our dreams and explored our fears.

When he moved out, I discovered that I would still have to conquer my greatest fear—letting him go. I saw that, in my heart, I was still picking him up and nursing him, holding him too tight, always afraid that I would turn around and he'd be gone. Perversely, in my drive to overcompensate for abandoning him, I have repeatedly tested his patience and tolerance, and yet he has continued to be loving and supportive. Gideon has reminded me many times that he considers himself lucky that I was so distracted while he was growing up. Otherwise, he says, he would never have developed the ability to make his own choices, to live his own life.

I want to keep taking care of Gideon, but I see that, in fact, since he was a little boy, he has been taking care of me. As I learn, painfully, slowly, to also turn that unconditional love inward, to forgive my inadequacies, recognize my successes and take responsibility for myself, perhaps it will become easier to trust that the bond that connects us is real and lasting.

In the twelve steps of Alcoholics Anonymous, steps eight and nine ask us to list those we have harmed and then make direct amends to such people. There is no compensation for the loss and injury that I have caused my son; there is no way to remake the past or undo the harm. So today I make living amends to Gideon by living a sober, safer life; he no longer has to take care of his mom. By loosening my suffocating grip on him, I am giving him the respect and unconditional love that he deserves and has always given me. I am also giving him the stories in this book, which are *our* stories, as imperfect and unfinished as our love for each other.

GOD

I have never been religious, and I have always believed in god.

My parents identified themselves as Jews but were not one bit observant. We celebrated Christmas until Mother married Mel, by which time I was also married and out of the house. My meager exposure to religion was through my grandparents' kosher household, Jewish summer camp activities and an occasional youth program at the local Unitarian Church, where I remember people talking about one god for everyone.

Like my parents, Grandma Frances was Jewish but not observant. She attended a convent school, and when I was a child told me wonderful stories about the nuns. I wanted to be a nun. I was intrigued by their dignified garments and could imagine nothing more comforting than living in closet-like quarters among protective, spiritual women.

I've never lost that fascination. I love any movie with a nun in it: *The Sound of Music, The Nun's Story, The Flying Nun, The Singing Nun,* even *Sister Act.* I've collected and made nun dolls. And the nuns (along with priests, rabbis, monks, bishops and other clergy) have been enormously supportive of A Place Called Home.

Sister Pat is one of my closest friends, not because she's a nun, but because she's wise, patient, funny, open-minded and deeply committed to making this a better world. Just as I look past the clothes and tattoos of the gangbangers, she sees through my worldly dramatics to the person inside. We are soul sisters.

God has always felt like a unifying force. Not an old white man with a long beard, but a giant, warm spirit, touching everyone.

Throughout my life, with its twists and turns, I have taken comfort in god's presence. This wasn't something I learned; it wasn't intellectual. It's a fact of my existence as straightforward as breathing. When I was abused or had cancer or struggled to recover from the accident, I never questioned god's existence or imagined that I had been abandoned.

As rooted as I am in the physical world, god, angels and spiritual forces of all kinds have always been my teachers and my guides. When I stopped drinking and started going to A.A., the notion of a higher power, turning my life and my will over to god, felt familiar and comfortable. It was another way of saying the same thing I had understood intuitively. Going to meetings, holding hands, praying to find sanity, all made sense, gave me hope and enabled me to share the burden of my personal pain with others who recognized it, as well as with a force greater than all of us.

To find that spiritual core is a miracle. It doesn't have to be A.A., Judaism, Buddhism, Islam, Catholicism or any other recognizable practice. But to find a place of peace, instead of the turmoil of self-recrimination, is an extraordinary, life-affirming experience. We can be born anything—perfect or damaged, Crip or Blood, Baptist or Zoroastrian—but what makes us something beautiful and special is our soul.

I'm open to anything that might help me get closer to that place of peace, whether it's going to temple, writing this book, seeing a therapist, weaving, doing yoga, praying, or sitting quietly. I'm open and I'm willing.

CAT TILT, DOG TILT

From my earliest days of doing Power Yoga with Bryan Kest, yoga has been a challenge, a reward and a healing force in my life.

Always energetic, I had skated, walked and run. I had tried tennis, Ping-Pong, kickboxing and every possible type of aerobic and gym workout. But nothing lasted long. I'd figure out the routine, compete (openly or inwardly) with the other participants and move on to something else.

Bryan introduced me to yoga, and he introduced yoga to South Central. I took Bryan's classes for several years. Then I stopped doing yoga and started jogging around South Central. I wanted to see where all my families lived. (During that time, I also stopped going to A.A. I was "too busy." Fortunately, I didn't drink.) I kept working out at the gym; the treadmill didn't require yoga's intense emotional and spiritual commitment.

When I resumed my yoga classes, I had a new instructor, Max Strom, who taught me new ways to breathe and work my body safely. When Max came to visit me at the hospital, I desperately wanted to show him that I could still stand on my head, and that I was still his most devoted student. Once I was home, working with Max helped to pull me into full recovery.

Right before the accident, one of my yoga friends had mentioned Ana Forrest. Her name is legendary in the yoga community. So after the accident, barely out of rehab, I decided that she needed to be my teacher. Hers was truly the hardest class I had ever taken.

Then, without waiting for my body to mend, I enrolled in Ana's teacher training program. I wanted to learn how to teach this amazing physical and spiritual practice. If Ana's "regular" classes were challenging, her teacher training was, for me, torture.

For two-and-a-half months in the summer, every Saturday and Sunday, all day long, we would watch, practice and do student teaching and critiques. It wasn't *doing* the yoga that was hard for me. It was the same demons that had dogged me throughout my school years: reading, writing papers, keeping records and remembering precise, orderly sequences of movements that would make sense to the yoga students.

The minute my turn would come, even when I knew exactly what I was supposed to do, even though I had rehearsed and studied, my mind would be blank. I did my eighteen sessions of student teaching at A Place Called

Home, where my yoga students said that they enjoyed the experience, but I felt like a failure. I couldn't complete my papers, and I didn't graduate from Ana's class.

But, just as I had persisted with my real estate licensing courses, a year later I signed up for Ana's teacher training again and started the same round of reading, reports and student teaching. I'd be called on to demonstrate three little poses, which I knew backward and forward, and I'd freeze up. The poses weren't hard; it was being called upon and immediately feeling Stupid. Even when I taught a pose successfully, I believed I had done it wrong, that I was without grace, once again a failure. I was unable to finish the course.

In Ana, I found a tough teacher and an inspired healer. We worked together physically and spiritually through many hours of private sessions. In the shelter of her focused, nonjudgmental support, I began to explore the wounds of my recent and distant past, including sexual abuse.

My yoga teachers—all of them—have had a huge impact on my personal growth and on my physical recovery. And beyond what they've done for me, they have each found a way to make an enormous contribution to A Place Called Home. Bryan taught classes to the children, including some of the toughest gang members, and has continued to be a major donor to APCH as well as giving us the proceeds from one of his classes every week for over ten years. Max made monetary and in-kind donations, providing our yoga students with mats and workout clothes. And semester after semester, Ana sends her teacher trainees to conduct their yoga classes at APCH.

For a while, when my doctors and friends told me that I wasn't allowed to stand on my head or do Downward Dog, I was furious. I stopped going to classes. But since my heart was repaired, I have gone back to yoga with a passion. I go to classes almost every day, and not in my usual habitual way, taking classes from the same teacher over and over (my way of creating a safe little closet in my yoga world). Now I take classes from many wonderful, inspirational teachers, and I sit right at the front of the room. I can feel that my brain is getting better; I can take in my teachers' words and process them in my body.

I am now a volunteer yoga teacher at A Place Called Home. During "Yoga in the Hood," I share with the mothers, the children and the staff all I have gained from my mentors over the years, as well as new positions and teaching techniques that I observe in my own daily practice. This is where I belong. Unlike during the teacher training, when I felt I couldn't remember anything and was frozen in front of the class, I am absolutely at ease. One of the mothers brought her infant to class with her. She was having a hard time holding the baby and doing the poses, so I simply took the baby in my arms and held it as I taught the class. I wasn't confused or flustered at all.

My teachers have each shown me a route to heaven. Yoga has given me another way to reach the children, to contribute to their lives and to heal my own.

FINDING FRIDA

Through the years, with occasional breaks, I have kept on weaving. For a while, Victoria and I had a business called "Sisters." I did the weavings and Victoria painted the frames around them. In 1992 we had a show of my handwoven portraits in Vic's beautiful frames.

The weaving always seems connected with hair cutting and takes me back to something I've loved since I was a teenager. Hair is every bit as varied in texture and color as yarn. When I cut Diana's cousin Flossie's hair, or Sister Pat's hair, it feels like weaving. When I weave, it's like playing with someone's hair.

Today I weave with the same passion. Though I no longer have the loom, I work on simple frames, stringing the warp between nails pounded into the wood, and setting the frame on an easel surrounded by my color-sorted bins of yarn. On request, I do portraits of children and dogs, but my most absorbing subject is Frida Kahlo.

Perhaps because my family was in the business, or because I'm a "visual" person, or because reading was always so difficult for me, some of my most profound influences have come from movies. In the movies *Sybil* and *The Burning Bed*, I saw my own disturbing story. In *Stand and Deliver*, I found inspiration that led to the opening of A Place Called Home. And in the movie *Frida*, I discovered an artistic and spiritual connection that drives me into the studio day after day.

While I still don't think of myself as an artist, I am inspired by Frida's art. Like Frida, I have been a political activist. She was in a serious accident, and I can certainly relate to that. She loved both men and women. She made fabulous statements with bold clothing. She spoke her mind. She married an artist. She wanted a baby so much. I was luckier, but my dream was to have six boys around the table.

On many levels, Frida is my inspiration. I have surrounded myself with her image—in books, clothing, jewelry, dolls and in my own weavings. The Frida weavings are getting much more detailed, and I feel Frida's power behind them. Translating *her* images into fiber, I give expression to my own emotions, my vision, and my pain. Weaving her story and writing my own, I illustrate my life.

FAT

Wendy, Victoria and I were each named and labeled at birth. I was Fat Stupid Ugly, Wendy was Beautiful Brilliant Talented, and Victoria was Normal. This cruel system not only denied our amazing richness and complexity as individuals and gave us each neurotic obsessions that would plague us from infancy onward, but it also served to drive a wedge between us, especially in our childhood. Fortunately, deep affection, time and a shared sense of humor have allowed us to see past each other's labels, even if we still struggle with our own.

I have fought against "Fat" my entire life. Through diets, drugs, bulimia and compulsive exercising, I have tried incessantly to reach an impossible goal: my father's approval.

Whatever its cost to my physical and psychological well-being, Preludin had not stopped me from feeling Fat. But once I had embarked on my fight against fat, I became an optimistic, habitual dieter.

Since I was twelve, I have been on every imaginable diet. Each one is a new solution that will work miracles. If I follow the rules, I'll get to my goal. Even if I've been on the same diet and it didn't work for me before, I'll start it again, convinced that *this* time it will work its magic. I cannot remember a time when I was not dieting. In fact, I really don't know how people eat if they're not following carefully delineated rules. In addition to the ever-popular Weight Watchers, Atkins, Jenny Craig and Zone diets, I have also spent interludes on, among a great many others, the Cantaloupe Diet, Lettuce Diet, Light Beer Diet, Cottage Cheese Diet, Grapefruit Diet, and Lettuce and Tomato Diet. In the full belief that they would make me shed pounds, I have consumed diet bagels, crackers, desserts, smoothies, pasta and anything else with the "D" word on the package. I have consulted nutritionists and acupuncturists, had my fat density measured and even forced myself into periodic bouts of bulimia. (My nutritionist recently cut me a deal: she'll donate $50 to A Place Called Home for every pound I lose.)

The only time I was ever thin enough was when I had cancer.

Besides assuring that I would do anything to avoid getting on a scale, this obsession with my size had several other effects on my life.

For one, it wasn't until I was in my fifties that, with Diana's patient help, I learned how to sit down at the table and eat a meal.

For another, I continue raiding the kitchen in the

middle of the night, while I am sound asleep. Diana would notice a bowl with the remains of what looked like strawberries or cereal in it sitting next to my bed, or she'd find me sleeping with a plate on my chest and cream cheese in my hair. She'd ask me: "Did you leave this? What is it?" I never had any idea. I had no memory of getting up, of eating, or of handling the food or the dishes.

All those years of dieting, sabotaged. Doctors and friends saying, oh, your metabolism must be so slow, you must not be doing this or that right. The reality is that no matter how many calories I cut out during the day, I was putting them right back in during the night.

I wouldn't believe Diana when she told me I had eaten something during the night. But one night I bit into an OxyClean tablet and gagged myself awake. That seemed to have cured me, but after a while I resumed my midnight rambling. Finally Diana called a locksmith and had locks installed on the kitchen doors. She hides the key.

Another effect of my fat obsession was that it completely distorted my self-image. Not only was I bigger than my family members, I always felt like the biggest person in any room, anywhere. At five foot four, I thought I was eye-to-eye with Gideon, Chris Smart and other people over six feet tall. I was also certain that I outweighed them.

Years ago, when I was working at Jon Douglas Company, there was a woman on my staff named Cookie. She was over six feet tall and weighed well over two hundred pounds, but was the *smallest* person in her family.

We would look at each other and feel like we were looking in a mirror—she saw herself as petite; I saw myself as a towering Amazon.

In my mind's eye, I am huge, an offensive linebacker. That's why I can fearlessly deal with gangbangers at A Place Called Home. It's why I can step into the middle of a fight and take a gun out of a gang member's hand. And it's why I'm always—*always*—dieting.

When I look at the family pictures, it's true, I *was* bigger than the rest of them, but not by a foot and a hundred pounds. Only recently have I been able to recognize that. I was shocked when my therapist, Sharon, showed me a tiny bottle of aspirin that was the same height as the difference between Victoria and me—two inches.

The sad truth is that I was never fat. In my baby book, Mother carefully recorded my weight and height—always well within the "normal" range. Hundreds and hundreds of photographs chronicle my life, and even I can see that, at worst, I was just a little chubby. I've been on a diet my entire life, lost and regained thousands of pounds, and the most I've ever weighed is ten pounds more than I do now.

Losing weight is a measure of my success. A pound makes all the difference. I gain a pound and sink into a self-loathing abyss; I lose a pound, and I'm capable of miracles.

I was born with ten fingers, ten toes and three labels: Fat, Stupid and Ugly. No matter what we do to change them, the labels we are given in childhood can only be ripped away with enormous pain, effort and clear-eyed determination. Through a lifetime of therapy, catastrophes and love, I have fought to function effectively in the world and searched for the balance point between my labels and my reality. And through this process, difficult as it has sometimes been, my lifelong labels have faded in intensity.

I will probably always be on a diet, but now when I go to a yoga class and find myself surrounded by slender, fit young bodies, I don't have to cover my belly or hide in the back of the room, and I don't have to see myself as Fat.

I know that I'm not a math whiz or a mechanical genius, that I mix up and make up words, that I'm dyslexic. But I also know that the people who love me understand. That if I say, "I'll be waiting *pantlessly*," they know that I don't mean I'm taking off my trousers, but that I'm waiting with bated breath. That doesn't make me Stupid.

I now understand that if I don't look like a magazine model, I'm not alone; very few people on the planet look like magazine models. We can be gorgeous without being perfect. I have learned to make the most of my appearance, turning my Ugly into an asset.

I'm not Fat, Stupid and Ugly. I'm Debrah.

WIFE

The accident forced me to reevaluate my entire life. My responsibilities at A Place Called Home, my traumatic personal history and my relationships with the people I loved were newly illuminated by my survival.

As oblivious as I was to the extent of my injuries when I returned home just a month later, one thing was immediately obvious: nothing would ever be the same. Nowhere was this more apparent than in my relationship with Diana.

Prior to the accident, our friendship had deepened over a period of several years. Together, we had discovered an entirely new level of trust, honesty and joy. We were already committed to each other when the violent intrusion of a drunken motorcyclist had nearly stolen our relationship and my life. We had had a potent demonstration of the fragility of life and a reminder that every moment mattered.

Freed from the ordeal of hospitals and rehab, neither of us had a very good idea of what lay ahead. Through the previous weeks, with undisguised love and iron-willed tenacity, Diana had nurtured me, protected me and refused to let me die. If our children had detected our love before, now it was obvious to a wider circle of family and friends.

Once we were home, we held on to the openness and intensity of our feelings. We were ready to let the universe know who we were, to openly acknowledge that we wanted to spend the rest of our lives together, and to share and celebrate our love in a ceremony of commitment among the people who were dear to us.

We began to make plans, gradually sharing our news. The reactions were warm, supportive and loving. No one seemed surprised; everyone was excited for us. We found a nondenominational minister, Traci, who helped us prepare. Before the ceremony, she encouraged us to go on a short retreat, a "pre-honeymoon," to write about and share our answers to a list of challenging questions about each other, life issues and spirituality. So we drove to Santa Barbara and had the honeymoon from hell. We spent most of the time with our arms crossed in front of our chests, fiercely defending our separate views on raising children. I forget how or why we got onto that topic, since our "children" were all in their late twenties and early thirties, but it obviously tapped into some lifelong sore spots in both of us. Determined to make our relationship work, we talked through our differences—a new experience for each of us—and came away feeling closer than ever.

On the evening of September 30, 1999, just four months after the accident, Diana and I celebrated our commitment at the New Otani Hotel in downtown Los Angeles. Our closest friends and family members sat on Chinese pillows in a circle around us as witnesses to our happiness. It was a beautiful ceremony, topped off by a miniature version of a fully decorated, three-tier wedding cake.

The next four years were almost impossibly difficult as I fought Diana's every effort to help me recover. It's a testament to the strength of our partnership that we survived, both individually and as a couple.

But because of and in spite of day-to-day battles, we were learning, growing and further enriching our relationship. The differences in our lives and lifestyles were significant, and one of the big issues for me was learning to travel. I hated to leave the security I felt in my own small house, which had replaced my closet. I could go to A Place Called Home or to yoga, do an occasional errand, and visit my one or two "safe" coffee shops and restaurants, but beyond that I just wanted to be home, in my room, with my animals. I rarely visited friends; they came to visit me. That was normal.

Until I met Diana. She always seemed to be going somewhere. She went to the theater, took classes, traveled and even went to other people's homes. What's more, she genuinely enjoyed doing these things. Diana was generous in her willingness to stay home with me, but only some of the time. If I wanted to be in this relationship, I would have to learn to leave the house with her. Step by step, I did.

Diana showed me that it was possible to travel *and* feel safe. Our first visit to New York was terrifying; I thought that the city would suck me right back into my horrible childhood. But now I love going to New York and all kinds of other places. It took me a long time to be able to say that I enjoyed leaving home. Sometimes I would resist out of habit, and sometimes I would go along just to make Diana happy, and that was okay, too. She made me feel safe in the world; it was the least I could do.

Another challenge of living with Diana was suddenly being part of a family. Family, and especially mealtime, was loaded with dangerous associations for me. Although I could serve dinner to five hundred people at A Place Called Home, the idea of sitting down at the table with family was terrifying—until Diana helped me see that there was nothing to fear.

Once we were officially a couple, Diana and I found ourselves hosting large gatherings. In addition to Gideon, my sister Victoria lived not far away with her husband and daughter. Diana's two beautiful daughters, their husbands, and the four adorable grandchildren were also nearby. Sometimes the circle expanded to include friends, other relatives and even Diana's ex-husband, his wife and his parents. When this crowd sat down together, the results were noisy and unruly, which at first was frightening to me. But eventually I came to understand that this was *happy* noise—that these people were talking and laughing, not tormenting each other. For the first time in my life, I began to feel like a normal human being, eating meals with Diana, sitting down every Tuesday night for family dinner.

We love these people, they love us, and to our great delight, they love each other. Phenomenally supportive, our families—both as individuals and as a group—have opened their hearts and their lives and embraced us, without hesitation and without judgment.

Diana and I had to create our relationship from scratch. We had no role models to rely upon and no rules to follow. As a couple, we each had our own past experiences in love and in life, good *and* bad, but no language for this new way of relating. Before the accident, our growing friendship had been fueled by the excitement of discovery. Although we had met challenges head-on, such as the aftermath of my relationship with Lewis, we were basically playmates. We talked, ate, shopped and laughed like schoolgirls. It was easy and unpressured.

But after the accident, now fully committed to each other, nothing was easy. Like any two people who live together, we faced "normal" day-to-day problems, but even the smallest concern was now fraught with an entirely new set of complications. I had brain damage but no capacity to understand it, and the dynamic of our relationship had shifted nearly 180 degrees. We were no longer equals; I was a balky teenager, and Diana had become my mom. We had to find our way back.

Our primary ally in that process was our therapist, Sharon Gedan. Week in and week out, individually and together, we took ourselves to her office. Progress seemed infinitesimal; sometimes there was no progress; sometimes we seemed to be slipping backward. But over time, Sharon helped us build our own tools for communication and showed us that our relationship could thrive without either of us sacrificing our needs or individuality.

Where our lives had previously told us to disguise or ignore our feelings (or withdraw into the closet), we now had to learn to trust, to share and to be open. Initially it was frightening and unsafe for both of us. We expected our needs to be met with criticism, punishment or mockery, but it never came.

Very gradually we got the hang of this new way of communicating, saying what was on our minds and going on to the next activity. I could tell Diana that I didn't like this or I didn't want to do that, and she never told me that I was Stupid; she could tell me that something made her angry, and I never turned my back on her. We didn't have to be perfect.

It didn't happen overnight. But we were (and are) so committed, so willing to do whatever was necessary, that we pushed our relationship to change. We fought our way back to being equals, respectful and loving, each taking responsibility for ourselves, encouraging the other, and guarding the rare and beautiful life we had discovered together. We no longer spend much energy or time on hiding our feelings. We get it out and move on. It's much more fun that way.

Diana learned to tolerate my competitiveness. Instead of being hurt, she laughs at me. I'll turn anything into a contest—who walks faster, who lost more weight this week. When Diana told me that she didn't want to go to Weight Watchers to be weighed in one day, I told her I'd quit if she didn't go; when we weighed in, I told her I'd quit because she'd lost a pound more than I had. I hate losing. We'd play Scrabble, and I'd turn letters over to look like blanks, pick out the letters I wanted and throw back the ones I didn't want—and that's even after I'd persuaded Diana to give me a fifty-point advantage because of my reading problem. She laughs.

We wake up laughing, and we go to sleep laughing. Giggling, we do a spot check in the morning on the dress for the day, making sure that the shoes match the skirts match the purses. With feigned sternness, we keep each other from cheating on our diets. Sometimes we laugh until our sides ache. Our shared sense of humor, our willingness to be goofy, continually benefits our survival as a couple. However difficult the issues of the moment, before long we're laughing again.

We are also unusually supportive of each other. In addition to our life together, we each have lives of our own. Diana is a wonderful artist, and I love watching her paint. I continually pester her to take more classes and spend more time in the studio. As a result, she takes her work more seriously and her skills have grown in great leaps.

Her time in the studio doesn't take anything away from me; it only enriches our relationship.

The same is true of the time we spend with our friends. Of course we do things as a couple, but Diana has her friends and family, and I have mine. We can independently spend a day, go out to dinner or take a class with someone else without feeling threatened. If the need arises, we can and do travel alone. We have given each other the freedom to be ourselves and to have complex and interesting lives. We use those as the ingredients to enrich our life together.

Sometimes we meet during the day for coffee or for lunch or at A Place Called Home. We're both so excited, you'd never know that we lived together, that we had seen each other just hours before. It's real love.

I've now known Diana for over eight years. When I met her, she didn't have any grandchildren; now she has four. There was no textbook to show us the right way to meet the challenge of my prolonged and medically complex four-year recovery, but we both survived. Diana has learned to love my animals, and I have learned to love being safe in her big noisy family. We continue to see our wonderful therapist, and we don't let problems fester. We know that we have a long way to go, but that's not depressing, it's exciting—we look forward to becoming little old ladies together.

As we were making the final changes to this book, Diana and I flew to San Francisco for a very short vacation. On March 1, 2004, we went to City Hall, where hundreds of couples were participating in an uplifting celebration of love that had taken the city—and the nation—by storm. We went to express our solidarity and to add our voices to the growing chorus in support of those who were taking this important step in their lives—and in the history of equal rights.

Couples from all over the country waited excitedly to get their marriage licenses. Then, clutching the precious piece of paper, many took their vows right on the spot. There were several ministers officiating in the waiting area and on the landings of the grand staircase in the rotunda of the building. An enormous wedding cake with the words "Congratulations on Your Marriage!" was set out for everyone to share.

Carrying an armload of bright, coral-colored roses, we walked from couple to couple, greeting them, congratulating them, and giving them flowers and hugs. The air was charged with laughter and tears shared as the unions were legitimized. Standing in the midst of all of these people publicly affirming their commitment to each other, we experienced a powerful spiritual connectedness. In sharing their love, Diana and I again acknowledged our own.

We are best friends, and we are both wives. I'm Diana's wife; she's my wife. Our hearts are open. Our love is unconditional. In each other, we have both found a place called home.

SACRED MUSIC

n 2002, I was honored as a "Local Hero" at the World Festival of Sacred Music. In a huge amphitheatre, before hundreds of people, musicians, singers and dancers from all over the world joined in a celebration of unity and peace.

The thoughts I shared with the audience that day seem an apt conclusion to this story:

> It is amazing to see how many different ways there are to express joy and hope.
>
> Every one of us—whether we're on the stage or in the audience or out on the streets—every single one of us can share in this expression.
>
> Even those of us who can't sing or don't dance or never picked up a musical instrument can add our spirit and our energy to the voices of hope.
>
> As we've seen here, hope has many voices.
>
> Hope is a chant, a chorus and a dance.

Hope is a child who discovers the magic of books.

Hope is a mentor who opens his life to a teenager from South Central.

Hope is a girl who, against all odds, earns a scholarship to college.

Hope is a volunteer who shows up week after week.

Hope is a gangbanger who learns to play guitar.

Hope is a shy and awkward youth who blossoms into a graceful dancer.

Hope helps us see beyond our boundaries.

It helps us wake up each day.

It helps us believe.

It keeps us coming back in the face of frustration and doubt.

It fuels our dreams.

Hope is a universal language.

It transcends the borders of neighborhood and country, of skin color and education, of age and religion.

Whether we work in a store or a school, an office tower or a field, hope helps us imagine a better future.

It helps us see the connection between education and tolerance, and lights the path between personal responsibility and peace.

Hope is very simply one person helping another.

Reaching out with love.

Opening our arms and our hearts to each other to share our blessings and our sorrows, our abundance and our need.

Joining our voices in a chorus of song, prayer or protest,
we give each other strength to face another day.
The people who make change happen are no different
from the rest of us.
They simply get up each morning and light the flame of
hope in their hearts, then go out and begin again the
hundreds of small tasks that make up each day.
In the language of hope, we are all equal.
Each one of us can lead as well as follow.
Each one of us can give as well as take.
Each one of us is wise as well as innocent.
We all have work to do and riches to share and dreams
to explore.
Fueled by hope, supported by one another,
we are *all* heroes.

Awards Earned by Debrah Constance and A Place Called Home (partial list)

1994   Zoe Christian Fellowship First Annual Unity Award

1994   American Legion Certificate of Appreciation

1994   State of California Legislature 46th District Woman of the Year

1995   California State Senate Certificate of Recognition

1996   City of Los Angeles Certificate of Appreciation

1997   President's Summit for America's Future 50 Outstanding Teaching Examples in the United States

1998   United Nations Development Fund for Women First Annual Remarkable Women Award (other honorees included Oprah Winfrey and Madeleine Albright)

1999   City of Los Angeles Certificate of Commendation

2000   California Community Foundation features Debrah Constance as one of "85 Unsung Heroes of the Non-Profit Community"

2000   Vision in Philanthropy Award, Jewish Community Foundation

2001   Ben and Jerry's Citizen Cool Award

2001   People's Champ Award

2001   Nonviolence in Our Community Award

2002   World Festival of Sacred Music Local Hero Award

2002   Returned Peace Corps Volunteers of Los Angeles Local Hero Award

2003   Los Angeles' Promise, The Alliance for Youth Five Promises' Award for Safe Places

ABOUT THE AUTHOR

Debrah Constance founded A Place Called Home (APCH) in 1993 in the basement of a church to give inner-city, gang-affected youth a place where they could come after school, get a snack, do their homework, watch TV, play with their friends and be with people who care about them—basic rights that all kids should have. From this fundamental concept, APCH grew at an exponential rate and now offers its youth members many programs, including an all-day school in collaboration with the Los Angeles Unified School District, computer lab, music, art, dance, tutoring and mentoring. In 1996, with a growth in membership to 400, APCH moved to its present location—a 10,000 square foot facility that today serves over 4,000 children.

For more information about A Place Called Home, go to *www.apch.org* or call 323-232-7653. Visit the author online at *www.fatstupidugly.com*.

J.I. Kleinberg is a California-based freelance writer.

NEW YORK TIMES BEST SELLERS!

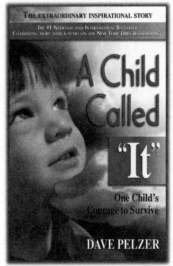

Through each struggle you'll find yourself enduring his pain, comforting his loneliness and fighting for his will to survive. This compelling story will awaken you to the truth about child abuse—and the ability we all have to make a difference.

Code 3669 • Paperback • $11.95

In the bestselling sequel to *A Child Called "It"*, Dave Pelzer answers questions and reveals new adventures through the compelling story of his life as an adolescent.

Code 5157 • Paperback • $12.95